I0005877

Apple
Watch
for Seniors

A Simple Step by Step Guide for Beginners

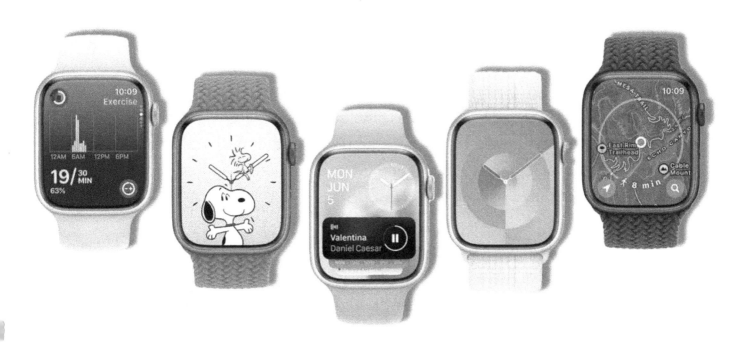

Jason Brown

Copyright © 2023 Jason Brown

All rights reserved. No part of this publication may be reproduced, distributed or transmitted in any form or by any means, including photocopying, recording, or other electronic or mechanical methods, without the prior written permission of the publisher, except in the case of brief quotations embodied in critical reviews and certain other non-commercial uses permitted by copyright law.

Trademarked names appear throughout this book. Rather than use a trademark symbol with every occurrence of a trademarked name, names are used in an editorial fashion, with no intention of infringement of the respective owner's trademark. The information in this book is distributed on an "as is" basis, without warranty. Although every precaution has been taken in the preparation of this work, neither the author nor the publisher shall have any liability to any person or entity with respect to any loss or damage caused or alleged to be caused directly or indirectly by the information contained in this book.

CONTENTS

UPDATE, BACKUP, RESTORE & RESET   135

APPS & ICONS

Audiobooks	Blood Oxygen	Calculator
Calendar	Camera Remote	Compass
Contacts	Cycle Tracking	ECG
Find Devices	Find Items	Heart Rate
Home	Mail	Maps
Medications	Memoji	Messages
Mindfulness	Music	Find Friends
Noise	Now Playing	Stopwatch
Photos	Podcasts	Voice Memos
Remote	Settings	Weather
Sleep	Stocks	Shortcuts
Timers	Tips	News
Walkie-Talkie	Wallet	Phone
Workout	World Clock	Reminders

Status Icon	What is Means
●	You have an unread notification. Swipe down on the watch face to read it.
⚡	Apple Watch is charging.
⚡	Apple Watch battery is low.
○	Low Power Mode is on.
🔒	Apple Watch is locked. Tap to enter the passcode and unlock.
💧	Water Lock is on, and the screen doesn't respond to taps. Press and hold the Digital Crown to unlock.
🌙	Do Not Disturb is turned on. Calls and alerts won't sound or light up the screen, but alarms are still in effect.
👤	Personal Focus is turned on.
🪪	Work Focus is turned on.
🛏	Sleep Focus is turned on.
✈	Airplane mode is turned on. Wireless is turned off but non-wireless features are still available.
🎭	Theater mode is turned on. Apple Watch is silenced and its display won't light up when you raise your wrist.
🏃	You have a workout in progress. To end the workout, see End and review your workout.
✕	Apple Watch with cellular has lost the connection to a cellular network. See Use your Apple Watch with a cellular network.

STATUS ICON	WHAT IS MEANS
	Apple Watch is connected to its paired iPhone.
	An app on Apple Watch is using location services.
	Apple Watch is connected to a known Wi-Fi network.
	There's wireless activity or an active process happening.
	The microphone is on.
	Apple Watch is connected to a cellular network. The number of green bars indicates signal strength.
	You've made yourself available to be reached on Walkie-Talkie. Tap the icon to open the Walkie-Talkie app.
	Apple Watch has lost the connection with its paired iPhone. This happens when Apple Watch isn't close enough to iPhone, or when airplane mode is enabled on iPhone. For more information, see the Apple Support article If your Apple Watch isn't connected or paired with your iPhone.

SETTING UP YOUR iWATCH

Introducing Your Apple Watch
Say hello to the Apple Watch, the adaptable wearable partner that can inspire you to enhance your activity levels, monitor vital health details, maintain connections with your loved ones, and offer numerous other capabilities, whether paired with your iPhone or used independently.
This manual is designed to unveil the multitude of incredible features that the Apple Watch has to offer, especially with watchOS 9.4.

Apple Watch gestures

You use several basic gestures to interact with Apple Watch.

Tap: Touch one finger lightly on the screen.

Swipe: Move one finger across the screen—up, down, left, or right.

Drag: Move one finger across the screen without lifting.

Setting Up and Connecting Your Apple Watch with iPhone
To utilize your Apple Watch with watchOS 9, it's essential to establish a connection between your watch and an iPhone 8 or a later model running iOS 16 or newer. During this process, both your iPhone and Apple Watch's setup assistants collaborate to facilitate the pairing and configuration of your watch.

Note: If you encounter visibility challenges with either your Apple Watch or iPhone, you can utilize VoiceOver or Zoom to assist you, even during the initial setup. Refer to the "Set up Apple Watch using VoiceOver or Zoom" guide for further details.

SETTING UP, PAIRING, AND CONFIGURING YOUR APPLE WATCH

1. Place your Apple Watch on your wrist. Adjust the band or select an appropriate band size to ensure a snug and comfortable fit.

2. To power on your Apple Watch, press and hold the side button until the Apple logo appears.

3. Bring your iPhone in close proximity to your Apple Watch. Wait for the Apple Watch pairing screen to display on your iPhone's screen, then tap "Continue."

Alternatively, you can launch the Apple Watch app on your iPhone and tap "Pair New Watch."

4. Choose the "Set Up for Myself" option.

5. As prompted, position your iPhone in such a way that your Apple Watch is visible within the viewfinder of the Apple Watch app. This action will establish a connection between the two devices.

6. Select "Set Up Apple Watch," and then follow the step-by-step instructions provided on both your iPhone and Apple Watch to complete the setup process.

ALL APPLE WATCHES BUTTONS AND LAYOUTS

Apple Watch Series 8

- Display
- Digital Crown
- Microphone
- Side button

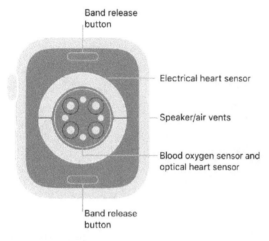

- Band release button
- Electrical heart sensor
- Speaker/air vents
- Blood oxygen sensor and optical heart sensor
- Band release button

Apple Watch Series 7

- Display
- Digital Crown
- Microphone
- Side button

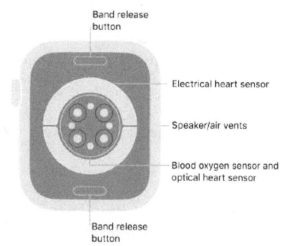

- Band release button
- Electrical heart sensor
- Speaker/air vents
- Blood oxygen sensor and optical heart sensor
- Band release button

Apple Watch Series 6

- Display
- Digital Crown
- Microphone
- Side button

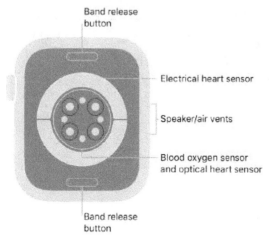

- Band release button
- Electrical heart sensor
- Speaker/air vents
- Blood oxygen sensor and optical heart sensor
- Band release button

Apple Watch SE (2nd Generation)

- Display
- Digital Crown
- Microphone
- Side button

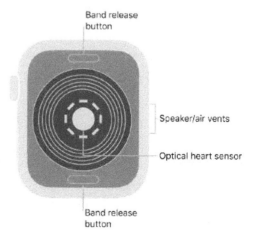

- Band release button
- Speaker/air vents
- Optical heart sensor
- Band release button

Apple Watch SE

- Display
- Digital Crown
- Microphone
- Side button

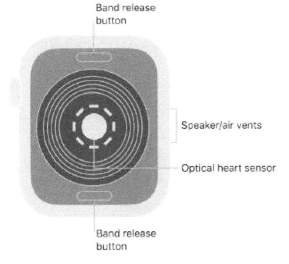

- Band release button
- Speaker/air vents
- Optical heart sensor
- Band release button

APPLE WATCH SERIES 4 AND SERIES 5

- Display
- Digital Crown
- Microphone
- Side button

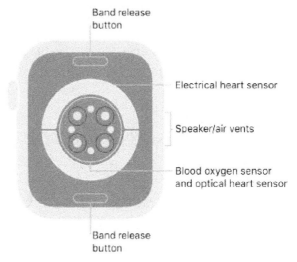

- Band release button
- Electrical heart sensor
- Speaker/air vents
- Blood oxygen sensor and optical heart sensor
- Band release button

THE APPLE WATCH APPLICATION

Utilize the Apple Watch application on your iPhone to personalize watch faces, configure settings and notifications, set up the Dock, install applications, and perform various other tasks. If you're interested in acquiring additional applications from the App Store, refer to the "Get more apps" section for detailed guidance.

ACCESSING THE APPLE WATCH APPLICATION

1. On your iPhone's home screen, tap the icon of the Apple Watch application.
2. Select "My Watch" within the application to access and modify the settings associated with your Apple Watch.

If your iPhone is connected to more than one Apple Watch, the settings corresponding to your active Apple Watch will be displayed.

EXPLORING FURTHER INFORMATION ABOUT APPLE WATCH

In the Apple Watch application, the "Discover" tab offers links to valuable Apple Watch tips, an informative overview of your device, and this user guide. All of this content is conveniently accessible on your iPhone.

Swipe to see your watch face collection.

Settings for Apple Watch.

CHARGING YOUR APPLE WATCH

SETTING UP THE CHARGER

1. Place your charger or charging cable on a level surface in a well-ventilated area.
   - The Apple Watch Magnetic Fast Charger to USB-C Cable (included with Apple Watch Series 7 and Apple Watch Series 8) or the Apple Watch Magnetic Charging Cable (for other models) is provided with your Apple Watch.
   - Optionally, you can also utilize accessories like the MagSafe Duo Charger or Apple Watch Magnetic Charging Dock (available separately).

2. Connect the charging cable to the power adapter (available separately).

3. Plug the power adapter into an electrical outlet.

INITIATING APPLE WATCH CHARGING

1. Gently position the Apple Watch Magnetic Fast Charger to USB-C Cable (included with Apple Watch Series 7 or later) or the Apple Watch Magnetic Charging Cable (included with earlier models) onto the back of your Apple Watch.

   Note: The concave end of the charging cable will magnetically attach to the back of your Apple Watch, ensuring proper alignment.

2. Your Apple Watch will emit a chime to indicate the commencement of charging (unless it is in silent mode). Simultaneously, a charging symbol ⚡ will be displayed on the watch face.
   - The symbol appears in red when your Apple Watch requires power, transitioning to green when charging is active.
   - If your Apple Watch is in Low Power Mode, the charging symbol will be yellow.

CHARGING PLACEMENT OPTIONS

   - You can charge your Apple Watch with its band open in a flat orientation or on its side.
   - If using the Apple Watch Magnetic Charging Dock or MagSafe Duo Charger, simply place your Apple Watch on the dock.

LOW BATTERY INDICATION

In situations where your battery level is significantly low, you might see an image of the Apple Watch Magnetic Fast Charger to USB-C Cable or Apple Watch Magnetic Charging

Cable, accompanied by a low battery symbol ⚡ on the screen.

Here is a guide on where to place all chargers for each Apple Watch.

Apple Watch Series 8

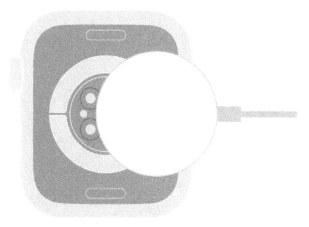

Apple Watch SE
(2nd Generation)

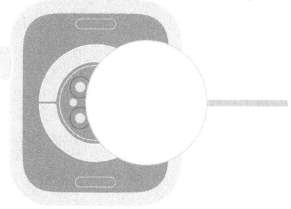

Apple Watch Series 7

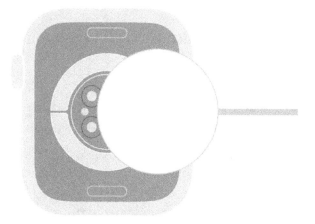

Apple Watch Series 6

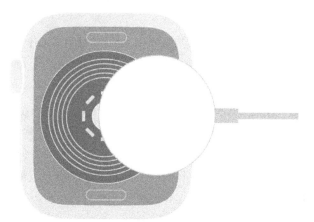

Apple Watch SE

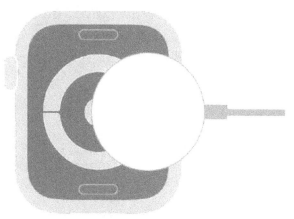

Apple Watch Series
4 & 5

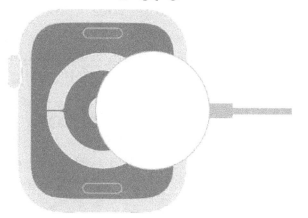

CHECK REMAINING POWER

To see remaining power, touch and hold the bottom of the screen, then swipe up to open Control Center. To more quickly check the remaining power, add a battery complication to the watch face.

View the percentage of remaining battery life.

CONSERVING BATTERY POWER

To extend your battery life, consider activating Low Power Mode. Enabling this feature will result in the deactivation of the Always On Display, background measurements of heart rate and blood oxygen levels, as well as heart rate notifications.

Some notifications might be delayed, emergency alerts could be delayed, and specific cellular and Wi-Fi connections may be restricted. Cellular functionality will remain inactive until you explicitly need it, such as when streaming music or sending messages.

Note: Keep in mind that Low Power Mode will automatically deactivate once your battery reaches 80% charge.

1. Touch and hold the bottom of the screen, then swipe up to open Control Center.
2. Tap the battery percentage, then turn on Low Power Mode.
3. To confirm your choice, scroll down, then tap Turn On Low Power Mode.
You can tap Turn On For, then choose On for 1 Day, On for 2 Days, or On for 3 Days.

Tip: If you've connected battery-powered devices like AirPods to your Apple Watch via Bluetooth, you'll find their remaining charge displayed on this screen. When the battery level descends to 10 percent or lower, your Apple Watch will notify you and present the option to enable Low Power Mode.

For comprehensive insights into Low Power Mode, refer to the Apple Support article titled "Use Low Power Mode on your Apple Watch."

Tip: To uncover strategies for optimizing battery longevity, explore the guide on "Maximizing Battery Life and Lifespan" available on the official Apple website.

RETURN TO REGULAR POWER MODE

1. Press and hold the lower portion of the screen, and then swipe upwards to unveil the Control Center.
2. Tap the battery percentage and deactivate Low Power Mode.

Monitoring Time Since Last Charge:

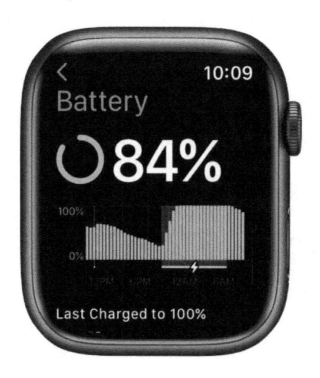

ACCESSING BATTERY INFORMATION

1. Launch the Settings app on your Apple Watch.
2. Select "Battery."

On the Battery screen, you'll find details such as the remaining battery percentage, a graphical representation illustrating recent battery charge history, and specifics regarding the time of the last charge.

CHECKING BATTERY HEALTH

You have the ability to determine your Apple Watch battery's capacity relative to its original state when new.

1. Open the Settings app on your Apple Watch.
2. Tap "Battery," and then navigate to "Battery Health."

Should your Apple Watch's battery capacity experience significant decline, the device will provide alerts, indicating that it may be time to explore available service options.

PREVENTING BACKGROUND APP REFRESH

When transitioning to a new app, the previous app doesn't remain actively open or occupy system resources. However, it might still refresh, checking for updates and new content in the background. Background app refresh activity can contribute to power consumption. To optimize your battery life, you can disable this feature.

1. Access the Settings app on your Apple Watch.
2. Navigate to "General," then select "Background App Refresh."

You can choose to deactivate "Background App Refresh" entirely, preventing all apps from refreshing, or customize the setting by scrolling down and turning off refresh for specific apps.

Note: Apps featuring complications on the current watch face will continue to refresh, even if their background app refresh setting is turned off.

TURN ON AND WAKE APPLE WATCH

POWERING ON AND OFF YOUR APPLE WATCH

Power On:
To activate your Apple Watch, hold down the side button until the Apple logo becomes visible (a brief black screen may appear before this).
The watch face will be displayed once your Apple Watch is turned on.

Power Off:
Typically, you'll keep your Apple Watch operational at all times. However, if you wish to power it off, follow these steps:

1. Press and hold the side button until the sliders emerge.
2. Tap the icon  positioned at the upper right corner.
3. Slide the Power Off slider to the right.

When your Apple Watch is powered off, you can press and hold the Digital Crown to view the current time.

ALWAYS ON

Enabling Always On Display Mode

For compatible Apple Watch models, the Always On feature ensures that your watch face and the current time remain visible even when your wrist is not raised. The moment you lift your wrist, your Apple Watch seamlessly resumes full functionality.

Note: When your Apple Watch is operating in Low Power Mode, the Always On Display is deactivated. To view the watch face, a simple tap on the display is sufficient.

Always On Display is accessible on Apple Watch Series 5, Apple Watch Series 6, Apple Watch Series 7, and Apple Watch Series 8.

Here's how you can configure Always On Display

1. Access the Settings app on your Apple Watch.
2. Choose "Display & Brightness," then select "Always On."
3. Activate Always On by toggling the switch. Additionally, you can fine-tune the following options:
   • Show Complication Data: Select the complications that will display data when your wrist is down.
   • Show Notifications: Choose which notifications will be visible while your wrist is down.
   • Show Apps: Decide which apps will remain visible when your wrist is down.

Waking the Apple Watch Display

By default, there are several ways to awaken your Apple Watch display:
   • Raising your wrist will initiate the display, and it will return to sleep mode when you lower your wrist.
   • Tapping the display or pressing the Digital Crown will have the same effect.
   • Rotating the Digital Crown in an upward motion will also wake the display.

If you prefer that your Apple Watch does not wake when you raise your wrist or turn the Digital Crown, follow these steps:
1. Launch the Settings app on your Apple Watch.
2. Navigate to "Display & Brightness."

3. Disable "Wake on Wrist Raise" and "Wake On Crown Rotation."

ADJUSTING CLOCK FACE RETURN DURATION

Modify the time it takes for your Apple Watch to revert to the clock face after exiting an app:
1. Launch the Settings app ⚙ on your Apple Watch.
2. Navigate to "General," and select "Return to Clock." Scroll down and pick the timing preference for your Apple Watch's return to the clock face:
   - Always
   - After 2 minutes
   - After 1 hour
3. Alternatively, press the Digital Crown to swiftly return to the clock face.

By default, the chosen setting applies to all apps. However, personalized times can be set for individual apps. To do this:
1. Tap an app on the same screen.
2. Select "Custom," and then pick the desired time duration.

RESUMING PREVIOUS ACTIVITY

For specific apps like Audiobooks, Maps, Mindfulness, Music, Now Playing, Podcasts, Stopwatch, Timers, Voice Memos, Walkie-Talkie, and Workout, you can configure your Apple Watch to return you to your last activity upon waking from sleep.
1. Access the Settings app ⚙ on your Apple Watch.
2. Go to "General," and choose "Return to Clock." Scroll down, tap the app you're interested in, and activate "Return to App."

To return to the clock face, simply halt the current activity within the app (e.g., pause a podcast, conclude a route in Maps, or cancel a timer).

For further control, you can also manage these settings through the Apple Watch app on your iPhone:
1. Open the Apple Watch app.
2. Tap "My Watch," proceed to "General," and then select "Return to Clock."

PROLONGING DISPLAY DURATION

Extend the time the display remains active upon tapping to wake your Apple Watch:
1. Launch the Settings app ⚙ on your Apple Watch.
2. Choose "Display & Brightness," then select "Wake Duration." Opt for "Wake for 70 Seconds."

LOCKING AND UNLOCKING YOUR APPLE WATCH

Unlocking Your Apple Watch

There are two primary methods for unlocking your Apple Watch: manual entry of the passcode or setting it to unlock automatically when your iPhone is unlocked.

• Manually Enter Passcode: To unlock your Apple Watch, wake it and then input the watch passcode.

• Unlock with iPhone: You can configure your Apple Watch to unlock automatically when you unlock your paired iPhone. To do this:
  1. Open the Apple Watch app on your iPhone.
  2. Tap "My Watch," proceed to "Passcode," and enable "Unlock with iPhone."

Please note that your iPhone must be within a standard Bluetooth range (approximately 33 feet or 10 meters) of your Apple Watch to facilitate automatic unlocking.

CHANGE YOUR PASSCODE

Modifying Your Apple Watch Passcode
If you wish to alter the passcode you initially established Apple Watch, adhere to these instructions:

1. Access the Settings app 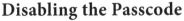 on your Apple Watch.
2. Tap "Passcode," then select "Change Passcode." Follow complete the process.

Alternatively, you can do this through the Apple Watch app on your iPhone:
1. Launch the Apple Watch app .
2. Tap "My Watch," navigate to "Passcode," and choose "Change Passcode." Follow the on-screen prompts to complete the procedure.

Disabling the Passcode
If you wish to deactivate your passcode, follow these steps:
1. Tap the Settings app on your Apple Watch.
2. Tap "Passcode," then select "Turn Passcode Off."

You can also achieve this via the Apple Watch app on your iPhone:

1. Open the Apple Watch app .

2. Tap "My Watch," navigate to "Passcode," and choose "Turn Passcode Off."

Note: If you disable your passcode will render Apple Pay unavailable on your Apple Watch.

AUTOMATIC LOCKING MECHANISM

By default, your Apple Watch will lock automatically when it's not being worn. To adjust the wrist detection setting, proceed as follows:

1. Launch the Settings app on your Apple Watch .

2. Tap "Passcode," then toggle the "Wrist Detection" option on or off.

Switching off wrist detection will impact the following Apple Watch functions:

• When authorizing an Apple Pay payment using your Apple Watch, you'll be prompted to input your passcode after double-clicking the side button.

• Certain Activity measurements won't be accessible.

• Heart rate tracking and notifications will be deactivated.

• The automatic locking and unlocking feature will be disabled.

• Even if a significant impact fall is detected, Apple Watch won't automatically initiate an emergency call.

FORGET YOUR PASSCODE

If you happen to forget your passcode, the solution involves erasing your Apple Watch. You can accomplish this through the following methods:

• Unpairing and Pairing: Detach your Apple Watch from your iPhone to wipe out both watch settings and the passcode. Subsequently, you can re-establish the pairing.

• Resetting and Pairing: Another option is to reset your Apple Watch and then pair it anew with your iPhone.

ERASE APPLE WATCH AFTER MULTIPLE UNLOCK ATTEMPTS

To safeguard your data in situations where your watch is lost or stolen, you can configure your Apple Watch to erase its content after 10 consecutive, incorrect passcode attempts.

1. Access the Settings app on your Apple Watch .

2. Tap "Passcode," then activate the "Erase Data" feature.

ADJUSTING LANGUAGE AND ORIENTATION ON APPLE WATCH

LANGUAGE OR REGION SELECTION

If you've configured your iPhone to support multiple languages, you can opt for the language displayed on your Apple Watch.

1. Access the Apple Watch app 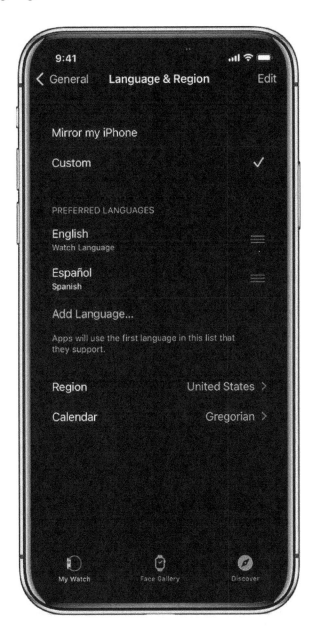 your iPhone.
2. Tap "My Watch," navigate to "General" > "Language & Region," then tap "Custom" and select your preferred language.

CHANGING WRIST OR DIGITAL CROWN PLACEMENT

If you wish to transfer your Apple Watch to your opposite wrist or prefer to have the Digital Crown positioned on the opposite side, you can modify your orientation settings. This ensures that raising your wrist triggers your Apple Watch and that turning the Digital Crown corresponds to your preferred direction.

1. Launch the Settings app  on your Apple Watch.
2. Navigate to "General" > "Orientation."

Alternatively, you can do this by using the Apple Watch app on your iPhone. Access "My Watch," proceed to "General," and select "Watch Orientation."

REMOVE, CHANGE, AND FASTEN APPLE WATCH BANDS

Ensure you choose a band that matches your Apple Watch case size. Bands meant for Apple Watch (1st generation) or Apple Watch Series 1, 2, and 3 can be used with Apple Watch Series 4, 5, SE, 6, 7, SE (2nd Gen), and 8, as long as their sizes are compatible. Bands for 38mm, 40mm, and 41mm cases are interchangeable, while those for 42mm, 44mm, and 45mm cases are also interchangeable.

Most bands created for Apple Watch Series 4, 5, SE, 6, 7, SE (2nd Gen), and 8 are suitable for prior watch versions. The Solo Loop and Braided Solo Loop bands are tailored for Apple Watch Series 4, 5, SE, 6, 7, SE (2nd Gen), and 8. Bands designed for early Apple Watch models are also compatible with Apple Watch Series 4, 5, SE, 6, 7, SE (2nd Gen), and 8.

DETACH AND REPLACE BANDS

1. Depress the band release button on your Apple Watch.
2. Glide the band to the side to detach it, then slide the new band into place.

Avoid applying excessive force when inserting a band. If you encounter difficulty while removing or inserting a band, press the band release button once more.

SECURE THE BAND

To ensure the best functionality, it's important for your Apple Watch to fit snugly on your wrist.

The underside of your Apple Watch requires contact with your skin to facilitate features like wrist detection, haptic notifications, and heart rate tracking. Wearing your Apple Watch with the correct fit—neither overly tight nor too loose, with some space for ventilation—enhances your comfort and enables the sensors to perform their tasks effectively. Furthermore, the sensors function optimally when the watch is worn on the top side of your wrist.

APPS ON YOUR IWATCH

OPEN APPS ON APPLE WATCH

Access Apps Easily
The Home Screen provides access to all your Apple Watch apps, while the Dock offers swift entry to your most frequently used ones. You have the option to include up to 10 preferred apps in the Dock for convenient access.

Opt for Grid or List Display
Customize how your apps are shown on the Home Screen by selecting between grid and list views. Here's how:
1. Press and hold on the Home Screen.
2. Select either Grid View or List View.

OPEN APPS FROM THE HOME SCREEN

Depending on your view, you will have different methods to access Apps.

In grid view: Tap the app icon. If you're on the Home Screen, turning the Digital Crown opens the app at the center of the display.

From the watch face, press to see the Home Screen.

Tap to open an app.

- In list view: Rotate the Digital Crown and tap an app.

Turn the Digital Crown to browse the apps.

Tap to open an app.

RETURNING TO THE HOME SCREEN

After using an app, press the Digital Crown once. To switch to the watch face (or in grid view, tap the Home Screen), press it again.
Swift App Switching
To swiftly access your most recently used app while in another app or viewing the watch face, double-click the Digital Crown.

ARRANGE APPS ON APPLE WATCH

Adjusting app placement in grid view is simple:
1. Press the Digital Crown on your Apple Watch to reach the Home Screen.
If you're in list view, hold the Home Screen and select Grid View.
Alternatively, open the Settings app on your Apple Watch, access App View, then opt for Grid View.
2. Long-press an app and choose Edit Apps.
3. Move the app to your preferred spot.
4. Conclude the process by pressing the Digital Crown.

Touch and hold an app, then drag to a new location.

REMOVE AN APP FROM APPLE WATCH

To remove an app from your Apple Watch, follow these steps:
- On the Home Screen, touch and hold.
- Tap Edit Apps and select the X next to the app's name.
- The app will be removed from your watch but remains on your paired iPhone, unless you delete it there as well.

In list view, you can also swipe the app left, then tap to remove it from your watch. Note that if you remove an app from your iPhone, it will also be deleted from your Apple Watch.

TO ADJUST APP SETTINGS

1. Launch the Apple Watch app on your iPhone.
2. Tap My Watch, then scroll to the installed apps.
3. Tap an app to modify its settings.
Keep in mind that restrictions you set on your iPhone can impact your Apple Watch, such as disabling the Camera app.

CHECK APP STORAGE

- Open the Settings app on your Apple Watch.
- Navigate to General > Storage.

Alternatively, you can access this information through the Apple Watch app on your iPhone under General > Storage.

ADDING APPS TO YOUR APPLE WATCH

Your Apple Watch comes with various pre-installed apps for communication, health, fitness, and time management. You also have the option to install third-party apps from your iPhone or download new apps from the App Store directly on your Apple Watch. All your apps are accessible from the Home Screen.

TO GET MORE APPS FROM THE APP STORE ON YOUR APPLE WATCH

1. Open the App Store app on your watch.
2. Turn the Digital Crown to explore featured apps.
   • Tap a category or "See All" below a collection to discover more apps.
3. To get a free app, tap "Get." To purchase an app, tap the price.

If you see a cloud icon ⌁ instead of a price, you've already acquired the app and can download it again without any charge. Note that some apps may require the iOS version on your iPhone as well.

For specific apps, use the search field at the top of the screen, or type using Scribble (available on Apple Watch Series 7 and Apple Watch Series 8). You can also explore popular app categories by selecting a category.

Keep in mind:
• When using cellular data on your Apple Watch, be aware of potential data charges.

• Scribble, a feature that lets you write on the screen, is available on Apple Watch Series 7 and Apple Watch Series 8, accessible by swiping up and tapping Scribble.

• Note that the availability of Scribble may vary depending on language settings.

INSTALL APPS FROM YOUR IPHONE

Your Apple Watch can automatically install apps from your iPhone if there's a corresponding watchOS app available. These apps will appear on your Home Screen. However, if you prefer more control over which apps are installed, follow these steps:
1. Open the Apple Watch app on your iPhone.
2. Tap "My Watch," then select "General."
3. Turn off "Automatic App Install."
4. Scroll down to "Available Apps" on the same page.
5. Tap "Install" next to the apps you want to have on your Apple Watch.

This way, you can ensure that only the apps you specifically choose are installed on your Apple Watch, giving you a more tailored and organized experience.

APPS

Use Apple's default apps & In-app features for entertainment, connectivity & productivity.

ACTIVITY APP

Stay Active with Apple Watch
Keep track of your daily activity with the Activity app ◎ on your Apple Watch. This app helps you monitor your movement throughout the day and encourages you to achieve your fitness goals. It tracks your standing frequency, movement, and exercise minutes. You'll notice three rings in various colors that sum up your progress. The objective is to minimize sitting, increase movement, and accomplish each ring's goal every day.

Your activity records are also stored in the Fitness app on your iPhone. After tracking at least six months of activity, you can view trend data for active calories, exercise minutes, stand hours, distance walked, cardio fitness, walking pace, and more. In the Fitness app, tap "Summary" and then navigate to "Trends" to see how your activity compares to your average.

START YOUR FITNESS JOURNEY

When setting up your Apple Watch, you'll be prompted to configure the Activity app. If you decide not to at that moment, you can do it later when you open the Activity app for the first time.

1. Open the Activity app ⊙ on your Apple Watch.
2. Swipe left to read about Move, Exercise, and Stand, then tap "Get Started."
3. Use the Digital Crown to input your sex, age, height, weight, and wheelchair usage.
4. Select your activity level and get moving toward a healthier you.

MONITOR YOUR PROGRESS

You can easily track your progress by opening the Activity app on your Apple Watch whenever you want.

The Activity app showcases three rings:
- The **red** Move ring illustrates active calories burned.
- The **green** Exercise ring highlights the minutes of brisk activity completed.
- The **blue** Stand ring indicates how frequently you stood and moved for at least one minute per hour.

If you've told the specified that you use a wheelchair, the blue Stand ring changes to the Roll ring, which tracks how often you rolled for at least one minute per hour.

By turning the Digital Crown, you can view your current totals. Continue scrolling to access a graph of your progress, your total steps, overall distance, workouts, and flights climbed. If a ring overlaps, you've surpassed your goal. Turn the Digital Crown and tap "Weekly Summary" to assess your performance for the week.

VIEW YOUR WEEKLY SUMMARY

1. Open the Activity app ⊙ on your Apple Watch.
2. Scroll to the bottom of the screen using the Digital Crown, then tap "Weekly Summary."

This summary includes your week's totals for calories, average calories, steps, distance, flights climbed, and active time.

ADJUST YOUR GOALS

If you feel that your activity goals are either too demanding or not challenging enough, you can modify them.

1. Open the Activity app ⊙ on your Apple Watch.

2. Scroll to the bottom of the screen using the Digital Crown, then tap "Change Goals."
3. Adjust a goal by tapping ● or ● , then proceed by tapping "Next."

Each Monday, you receive notifications about the previous week's achievements and can tailor your goals for the upcoming week. Your Apple Watch recommends goals based on your past performance.

REVIEW YOUR ACTIVITY HISTORY

1. Open the Fitness app on your iPhone and tap "Summary."
2. Within the Activity section, tap ▦ and select a date to review your activity for that day.

Check Your Trends & Track Your Progress Over Time

The Fitness app on your iPhone offers valuable insight into your progress over time through the Trends section, which provides daily trend data for active calories, exercise minutes, stand hours, walking distance, stand minutes, cardio fitness, walking pace, and running pace. Trends compare your activity over the past 90 days with the previous 365 days.

To assess your trend and make improvements, follow these simple steps:

1. Launch the Fitness app on your iPhone and tap "Summary."
2. Swipe up to access the trends section.
3. If you're interested in reversing a trend, tap "Show More."
4. To review the history of a specific trend, tap on it.

When the Trend arrow for a specific metric points upward, it indicates that your fitness levels are being maintained or improved. Conversely, if the arrow points downward, your 90-day average for that metric is declining. To inspire you to reverse the trend, you'll receive coaching tips, such as "Walk an extra quarter of a mile a day."

View Your Achievements

Your Apple Watch rewards you with various awards for achieving personal records, maintaining streaks, and reaching significant milestones. To access your collection of awards, which includes Activity Competition awards and awards you're currently working towards, follow these steps:

1. Open the Activity app ⊙ on your Apple Watch.
2. Swipe left twice to reach the Awards screen.
3. Scroll down to view your awards. Tap an award to get more information about it.

Alternatively, you can access your awards through the Fitness app on your iPhone. Simply tap the Summary tab and swipe up to find Awards at the bottom of the screen.

For details on participating in competitions with friends, refer to "Compete with your friends."

MANAGE ACTIVITY REMINDERS

Activity reminders can be invaluable in helping you meet your goals. Your Apple Watch keeps you informed about your progress and alerts you if you're lagging behind your activity targets. To customize which reminders and alerts you want to receive, use these instructions:

1. Open the Settings app ⚙ on your Apple Watch.
2. Tap on "Activity," then configure your desired notifications.

You can also make these adjustments through the Apple Watch app on your iPhone. Open "My Watch," then tap "Activity."

PAUSE DAILY COACHING

If you prefer to temporarily deactivate activity reminders, follow these steps:

1. Open the Settings app ⚙ on your Apple Watch.
2. Tap "Activity," then toggle off "Daily Coaching."

You can also manage this setting via the Apple Watch app on your iPhone by navigating to "My Watch," tapping "Activity," and turning off "Daily Coaching."

ALARMS APP

SETTING ALARMS

Creating an alarm on your Apple Watch is a simple way to receive sound or vibration notifications at specific times. Here's how you can do it:

1. Use Siri : Command Siri by saying something like, "Set a repeating alarm for 6 a.m."

2. Manually Set an Alarm:
   a. Open the Alarms app 🕐 on your Apple Watch.
   b. Tap "Add Alarm."
   c. Choose between AM or PM, then select the desired hours and minutes. Note that this step isn't necessary when using the 24-hour time format.
   d. Adjust the time by turning the Digital Crown, then tap ✓.
   e. To activate or deactivate the alarm, tap the corresponding switch. Alternatively, tap the alarm time to customize options such as repeat, label, and snooze settings.

Note: If you prefer an alarm that silently vibrates your wrist without sound, enable silent mode.

AVOID THE SNOOZE BUTTON

When an alarm goes off, tapping the Snooze button grants you a few extra minutes before the alarm resounds. If you'd like to remove the snooze option, follow these steps:

1. Launch the Alarms app 🕐 on your Apple Watch.
2. Tap the alarm from the list of alarms, then switch off Snooze.

MANAGING ALARMS

Removing or adjusting alarms on your Apple Watch is easy. Follow these steps to handle your alarms effectively:

Deleting an Alarm:
1. Launch the Alarms app ⏰ on your Apple Watch.
2. Tap the alarm from the list.
3. Scroll down and tap "Delete."

Skipping a Wake-Up Alarm:
If you have a wake-up alarm as part of your sleep schedule, you can skip it for that evening:
1. Open the Alarms app ⏰ on your Apple Watch.
2. Tap the wake-up alarm listed under Sleep | Wake Up.
3. Choose "Skip for Tonight."

SYNCING ALARMS BETWEEN IPHONE AND APPLE WATCH

You can have the same alarms on both your iPhone and Apple Watch for consistent reminders:
1. Set the alarm on your iPhone.
2. Open the Apple Watch app ⬛ on your iPhone.
3. Tap "My Watch," then tap "Clock," and enable "Push Alerts from iPhone."

With these steps, you can effectively manage your alarms on both your Apple Watch and iPhone. Your Apple Watch will alert you when alarms go off, allowing you to snooze or dismiss them directly from your watch. Please note that your iPhone won't alert you when alarms on your Apple Watch are triggered.

AUDIOBOOK

Listening to audiobooks on your Apple Watch is simple. Follow these steps to add and play audiobooks:

ADDING AUDIOBOOKS

1. Launch the Apple Watch app  on your iPhone.
2. Tap "My Watch," then choose "Audiobooks."
3. Select "Add Audiobook" and pick the audiobooks you want to sync with your Apple Watch.

AUDIOBOOK STORAGE AND SYNC

- Your currently playing audiobook and the one listed below "Want to Read" will sync to your Apple Watch if there's space available.
- Up to five hours from each audiobook you add will also be downloaded to your watch when space permits.
- Audiobooks sync to your watch when it's connected to power.

PLAYING AUDIOBOOKS

1. Connect your Bluetooth headphones or speakers to your Apple Watch.
2. Open the Audiobooks app on your watch.
3. Scroll through the artwork using the Digital Crown.
4. Tap an audiobook to start playing it.

You can easily add and enjoy your favorite audiobooks on your Apple Watch. Remember that only audiobooks from Apple Books can be synced to your watch.

Playing and Controlling Audiobooks from your library

You can easily play and control your audiobooks on your Apple Watch. Here's how:

Streaming Audiobooks from Library:

1. Ensure your Apple Watch is near your iPhone or connected to Wi-Fi/cellular network (for cellular models).
2. Open the Audiobooks app  on your Apple Watch.
3. Tap "Library" and select an audiobook to start playing it.

Using Siri to Play Audiobooks
You can use Siri to start playing an audiobook. Just say, "Play the audiobook 'In the Time of the Butterflies.'"

Controlling Playback
- Adjust the volume by turning the Digital Crown.
- Use playback controls to pause, resume, skip forward, or go back.

▷	Play the audiobook.
❙❙	Pause playback.
⟳15	Skip ahead 15 seconds.
⟲15	Skip back 15 seconds.
1x	Playback speed. Options include 1x, 1 1/4x, 1 1/2x, 1 3/4x, 2x, and 3/4x.
☰	Choose a track or chapter.

BLOOD OXYGEN

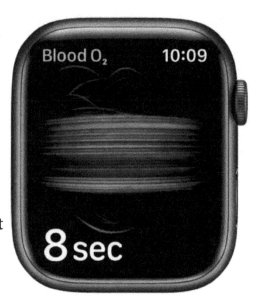

Measuring Blood Oxygen Levels with Apple Watch

You can use the Blood Oxygen app ⓘ on your Apple Watch Series 6 or later to measure the percentage of oxygen that your red blood cells carry from your lungs to the rest of your body. This measurement can provide insights into your overall health and well-being. Keep in mind that the Blood Oxygen app's measurements are not meant for medical use and may not be available in all regions.

SETTING UP BLOOD OXYGEN MEASUREMENTS

1. Open the Settings app ⚙ on your Apple Watch.
2. Tap "Blood Oxygen" and toggle on "Blood Oxygen Measurements."

DISABLING BACKGROUND MEASUREMENTS IN SPECIFIC MODES

When using Sleep Focus or theater mode, you might want to turn off background blood oxygen measurements to avoid distraction from the bright red light that shines against your wrist.
1. 1. Open the Settings app ⚙ on your Apple Watch.
2. 2. Tap "Blood Oxygen" and toggle off "In Sleep Focus" and "In Theater Mode."

The Blood Oxygen app ⓘ on your Apple Watch can periodically measure your blood oxygen level throughout the day if you have background measurements turned on. Additionally, you can manually take an on-demand measurement whenever you want.

STEPS TO TAKE AN ON-DEMAND BLOOD OXYGEN MEASUREMENT

1. Open the Blood Oxygen app ⓘ on your Apple Watch.
2. Place your arm on a table or your lap, ensuring your wrist is flat and the Apple Watch display is facing upward.
3. Tap "Start" and hold your arm very still during the 15-second countdown.
4. Once the measurement is complete, you'll receive the results. Tap "Done."

VIEWING YOUR BLOOD OXYGEN MEASUREMENTS HISTORY

1. Open the Health app ♥ on your iPhone.
2. Tap "Browse," then go to "Respiratory" and select "Blood Oxygen."

CALCULATOR

Using the Calculator App on Your Apple Watch

The Calculator app on your Apple Watch allows you to perform basic arithmetic calculations and provides quick tools for calculating tips and splitting bills.

QUICK CALCULATION

1. Open the Calculator app ⬚ your Apple Watch.
2. Tap the numbers and operators to perform calculations and get results.

CALCULATING TIPS AND SPLITTING BILLS

1. Open the Calculator app ⬚ on your Apple Watch.
2. Input the total amount of the bill.
3. Tap the "Tip" option.
4. Use the Digital Crown to select the desired tip percentage.
5. Tap "People" and use the Digital Crown to enter the number of individuals sharing the bill.

You will see the calculated tip amount, the overall total including the tip, and the individual amount each person needs to contribute if the bill is divided equally.

You can also utilize Siri to perform calculations by speaking your query aloud, such as "What's 73 times 9?" or "What's 18 percent of 225?"

The Calculator app on your Apple Watch offers quick and convenient tools for performing calculations, calculating tips, and splitting bills among friends or family.

CALENDAR

Checking and Managing Your Calendar on Apple Watch

The Calendar app on your Apple Watch allows you to access and manage your scheduled events, both in the near future and further ahead. Here's how you can use the Calendar app on your Apple Watch:

VIEW CALENDAR EVENTS

1. Open the Calendar app ^{Wed} 7 on your Apple Watch or tap the date or an event on the watch face.
2. Turn the Digital Crown to scroll through your upcoming events.
3. Tap an event to view its details, including time, location, invitation status, and notes.
   - To return to the next event, tap the "<" symbol in the top-left corner.

CALENDAR DISPLAY RANGE

The Calendar app ^{Wed} 7 on your Apple Watch displays events from the past six weeks and up to two years into the future in List and Day view.
The app can show events from all calendars on your iPhone or only the ones you choose. You can configure this setup on your iPhone using the Calendar app settings.

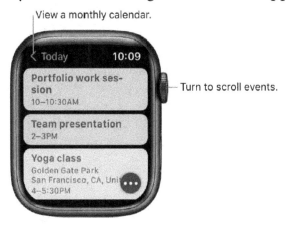

View a monthly calendar.

Turn to scroll events.

SIRI INTEGRATION

You can also use Siri to interact with your calendar events. For example, you can ask Siri, "What's my next event?" to get information about your upcoming schedule.

SWITCHING BETWEEN WEEKLY AND MONTHLY VIEWS

The Calendar app on your Apple Watch offers different viewing options to help you easily navigate through your events and appointments. Here's how you can change the way you view your calendar:

1. 1. Open the Calendar app on your Apple Watch.
2. 2. Tap the icon that looks like four small squares ().
3. 3. Choose from the available viewing options:
   - - Up Next: Displays your upcoming events for the week.
   - - Day: Shows events specifically for the current day.
   - - List: Presents a comprehensive list of all your events from the past two weeks to the next two years.

Navigating Within Views
- - In Day view: Swipe left or right to move to different days.
- - In List view or Up Next view: Turn the Digital Crown to navigate through your events.

RETURNING TO CURRENT DAY AND TIME:

To quickly jump back to the current day and time, tap the current time displayed in the top-right corner of the screen.

VIEWING WEEKS AND MONTHS:

While in Day or List view, you can also access week and month views.
- To show the current week: Tap the "<" symbol in the top-left corner.
- To view a different week: Swipe left or right.
- To select a specific week's events: Tap a day on the weekly calendar.
- To show the current month while viewing the current week: Tap the "<" symbol in the top-left corner.
- To view a different month: Turn the Digital Crown.
- To choose a week in the monthly calendar: Tap the desired week.

MANAGING EVENTS ON APPLE WATCH

The Calendar app on your Apple Watch allows you to effortlessly manage your events, create new ones, respond to invitations, and even get directions to event locations. Here's how you can perform various tasks related to events:

Adding an Event
Events you create on your iPhone's Calendar app are automatically synced to your Apple Watch.
1.   1. Use Siri: Say a command like "Create a calendar event titled Meeting with John for tomorrow at 2 p.m."
2.   2. Use the Calendar app on Apple Watch
- - While in Up Next, Day, or List view, tap the "Add Event" button ().
- - Fill in event details such as title, description, date, time, invitees, and choose the calendar.
     - Tap "Add" to create the event.

Deleting or Changing an Event
- Tap the event, then tap "Delete" and confirm the deletion.
- For recurring events, you can choose to delete just the selected instance or all future occurrences.
- To make changes to an event, use the Calendar app on your iPhone.

RESPONDING TO CALENDAR INVITATIONS

- If you see the invitation notification immediately, tap "Accept," "Decline," or "Maybe" at the bottom.
- If you come across the notification later, tap it in your notifications list, then respond.
- If you're in the Calendar app, simply tap the event to respond.

Contacting an event organizer
In the event details, tap the organizer's name, then use the available communication options like phone, message, email, or Walkie-Talkie.

Getting Directions to an Event Location if an event includes a location:
1. Open the Calendar app 7 on your Apple Watch.
2. Tap the event, then tap the address.
3. Your Apple Watch can provide directions to the event's location.

CAMERA REMOTE

Using Camera Remote and Timer on Apple Watch

Your Apple Watch can serve as a handy tool for capturing photos remotely and setting up the perfect shot. Whether you want to take a picture from a distance, adjust the frame, or set a timer, your Apple Watch can assist you. Here's how you can utilize the Camera Remote and Timer features.

Choose options.

Take a photo.

USING CAMERA REMOTE

Camera Remote allows you to control your iPhone's camera using your Apple Watch.

Ensure that your Apple Watch is within Bluetooth range of your iPhone (approximately 33 feet or 10 meters).

To initiate the Camera Remote function
1. Open the Camera Remote app on your Apple Watch.
2. Position your iPhone for the desired shot, using your Apple Watch as a viewfinder.
3. Utilize the Digital Crown to zoom in or out.
4. Adjust exposure by tapping the key area of the shot on your Apple Watch's preview.
5. When ready, tap the Shutter button on your Apple Watch to capture the photo.
   - The photo is saved in your iPhone's Photos app, but you can review it on your Apple Watch.

REVIEWING PHOTOS ON APPLE WATCH

After capturing a photo using Camera Remote, you can review it directly on your Apple Watch:

- Tap the thumbnail in the bottom left to view the photo.
- Swipe left or right to navigate through other photos.
- Turn the Digital Crown to zoom in further.
- Drag on a zoomed photo to pan.
- Double-tap a photo to fill the screen.
- Tap the screen to show or hide the Close button and shot count.

Tap Close when you're done reviewing.

USING TIMER

The Timer feature helps you set a delay for taking a photo, allowing you to get ready for the shot.

To set a timer:
1. Open the Camera Remote app 📷 on your Apple Watch.
2. Tap •••, then customize the timer's settings, camera, flash, Live Photo, and HDR options.

These features can help capture the perfect shot using your iPhone's camera while using your Apple Watch as a remote control while ensuring you're included in your photos even when you're behind the lens.

COMPASS

Using the Compass App ⅄ on Apple Watch
The Compass app on Apple Watch provides you with information about your direction, location, and elevation.

Note: If you're using Apple Watch SE or Apple Watch Series 5 or later, you can take advantage of additional features like Compass Waypoints and Backtrack for navigation.

VIEWING BEARINGS, ELEVATION, INCLINE, AND COORDINATES

- The center of the watch face displays your bearing.
- Scroll the Digital Crown to reveal information about incline, elevation, and coordinates on the inner compass ring.
- Further scrolling shows waypoints' locations if you've created any.
- To access a list view for details, tap at the top left.

Adding, Editing, and Clearing Bearings:

Open the Compass app ⅄ on your Apple Watch.

To add a bearing
- Tap ☰, scroll down, and choose Bearing.
- Use the Digital Crown to set the bearing, then tap Done.

To edit a bearing:
- Tap ☰, scroll down, and select Bearing.
- Adjust the bearing using the Digital Crown, then tap Done.

To clear a bearing:
- Tap ☰, scroll down, and tap Clear Bearing, then tap Done.

TO USE TRUE NORTH INSTEAD OF MAGNETIC NORTH

Open the Settings app ⚙ on your Apple Watch.

Tap Compass, then turn on Use True North.

You can also select a grid system, such as DMS, decimal degrees, MGRS/USNG, or UTM, through the Compass settings screen.

CREATING AND VIEWING COMPASS WAYPOINTS

If you have an Apple Watch SE or Apple Watch Series 6 with watchOS 9 or later, you can utilize Compass Waypoints in the Compass app. Compass Waypoints allow you to mark your current location and determine the distance and direction to each waypoint you set up.

Here's how to use Compass Waypoints:

1. Open the Compass app 🧭 on your Apple Watch.
2. Tap the 📍 symbol to add a new waypoint.
3. Provide details for the waypoint, such as a label, color, or symbol (like car or home). Once you're done, tap Done.
4. To view a Compass Waypoint:
- Tap on any of the three Compass screens.
- Use the Digital Crown to select the desired waypoint.
- Tap Select.
  The screen will display the distance and direction to the waypoint, for instance, "3.7 miles to your left."
5. You can tap the bottom of the screen to see the waypoint on a map, complete with its coordinates.
6. If you need to edit information about a waypoint, tap ⊘ on the waypoint screen.

FIND YOUR WAY BACK

On your Apple Watch SE or Apple Watch Series 6, equipped with watchOS 9 or newer, you can utilize the Compass app to help you retrace your route and navigate back to your starting point, particularly when you're in unfamiliar areas.

Please note that the Backtrack feature is designed for use in remote environments—such as locations far from your usual places like home or work—and in areas with limited Wi-Fi coverage.

Here's how to retrace your steps using the Compass app:

1. Open the Compass app ⚲ on your Apple Watch.
2. Tap 👣, and then press Start to initiate the recording of your route.
3. When you wish to retrace your steps, tap ⏸ and choose Retrace Steps. The compass will guide you towards your original starting point.
4. Follow the path displayed on the compass to navigate back to where you initially activated Backtrack.
5. Once you've reached your original starting point, you can conclude the process by tapping 👣 and selecting Delete Steps.

The Backtrack feature can be a handy tool when you need to navigate back to your original location, offering a sense of security and guidance when exploring unfamiliar surroundings.left corner of the camera app. It will open your recently taken photos and videos on your iPhone. Swipe through the photos and videos to view your recently taken shots. Tap "All Photos" at the top right corner to view your photos in the Photo app.

CONTACTS

Within the Contacts app ou can efficiently manage, edit, and share your contacts, ensuring seamless communication across your devices linked to the same Apple ID. Here's how to navigate and make the most of this app on your Apple Watch

VIEW AND INTERACT WITH CONTACTS

1. Open the Contacts app on your Apple Watch.
2. Use the Digital Crown to scroll through your contacts list.
3. Tap a contact to access detailed information and any accompanying notes.

EFFORTLESS COMMUNICATION

You can easily initiate various forms of communication directly from the Contacts app.

1. Open the Contacts app on your Apple Watch.
2. Scroll through your contacts using the Digital Crown.
3. Select a contact, then choose from the following options:
- Tap 📞 view the contact's phone numbers. Tap a number to make a call.
- Tap 💬 to access existing message threads or start a new one.
- Tap ✉ to compose an email.
- Tap ⊙ to send an invitation for Walkie-Talkie or, if they've already accepted and enabled Walkie-Talkie, start a conversation.

CREATING A NEW CONTACT

1. Open the Contacts app on your Apple Watch.
2. Swipe downwards, then tap New Contact.
3. Enter the contact's name and, if relevant, company information.
4. Include a phone number, email address, and physical address as needed, then tap Done.

SHARING, EDITING, OR REMOVING CONTACTS

1. Open the Contacts app on your Apple Watch.
2. Scroll through your list of contacts using the Digital Crown.
3. Choose a contact, scroll down, and then tap Share Contact, Edit, or Delete Contact, depending on your intention.

CYCLE TRACKING

Stay Informed with Cycle Tracking

With the Cycle Tracking app 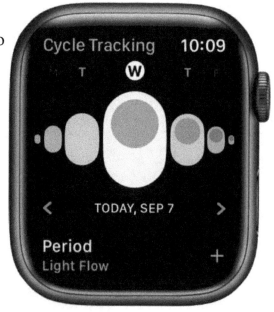, managing your menstrual cycle becomes effortless. You can easily log crucial details such as flow information and symptoms like headaches or cramps. This app uses the logged data to predict the start of your next period or fertile window, sending you timely alerts. Plus, when you pair this information with heart rate data, the Cycle Tracking app's predictions become even more accurate. If you wear an Apple Watch Series 8 during sleep, the app can utilize wrist temperature for enhanced period predictions and retrospective ovulation estimates.

SAFEGUARDING YOUR PRIVACY

The Health app ensures your data remains secure and empowers you to control what information you share. Your privacy is a top priority, and the Health app is built with that principle in mind.

SETTING UP CYCLE TRACKING

1. Open the Health app ♥ on your iPhone.
2. Tap Browse located at the lower right, bringing up the Health Categories screen.
3. Find and tap on Cycle Tracking.
4. Initiate the process by tapping Get Started, then follow the onscreen instructions to configure notifications and other preferences.

TRACK YOUR MENSTRUAL CYCLE WITH APPLE WATCH

1. Launch the Cycle Tracking app on your iPhone.
2. Utilize the available buttons and selection options to details, such as flow level and symptoms.

ECG

Apple Watch Series 4 or a newer model, can utilize the built-in electrical heart rate sensor and the ECG app ⩗ to perform an electrocardiogram. This feature allows you to monitor your heart's electrical activity and gain insights into your cardiac health.

Please note that the ECG app requires your iPhone to be updated to at least iPhone 8 or a later version of iOS, and your Apple Watch needs to be running the latest version of watchOS. It's important to know that the ECG app is not available on Apple Watch SE and might not be accessible in all regions.

TO RECORD AN ECG

1. Open the Health app ♥ on your iPhone. Follow the onscreen instructions to set up the ECG feature. If you don't see a setup prompt, access the Health app, tap Browse at the bottom right, then navigate to Heart > Electrocardiogram (ECG).
2. On your Apple Watch, launch the ECG app.
3. Find a comfortable position by resting your arm on a table or in your lap.
4. Use the hand opposite your watch and place your finger on the Digital Crown. Wait as your Apple Watch records the ECG. It's important to note that during the session, you don't need to press the Digital Crown.

This simple process allows you to perform an ECG conveniently and gain valuable insights into your heart's electrical activity.

After the recording is complete, you will receive a classification of the recorded ECG. To further enhance the details, you have the option to tap "Add Symptoms" and select any relevant symptoms you may be experiencing. Once you've chosen your symptoms, tap "Save" to include these notes, and then tap "Done" to complete the process.

To review your ECG results on your iPhone, open the Health app ♥, tap "Browse" at the bottom right, and then navigate to "Heart" > "Electrocardiograms (ECG)."

USE FIND PEOPLE, DEVICES, AND ITEMS

Discover the whereabouts of your loved ones with your Apple Watch

The Find People app  provides a convenient means to locate and stay connected with people who hold significance in your life. By utilizing this app, you can find the location of individuals who share their location with you. As long as your friends and family members use iPhone, iPad, iPod touch, Apple Watch SE, or Apple Watch Series 4 or later, they will appear on a map, enabling you to swiftly pinpoint their positions. You also have the option to set up notifications that inform you when your acquaintances arrive at or depart from specific places.

ADD SOMEONE TO YOUR CIRCLE

1. Launch the Find People app on your Apple Watch.
2. Scroll down and tap "Share My Location."
3. Choose a contact using either Dictation, Contacts, or Keypad.
4. Pick an email address or phone number associated with that contact.
5. Determine the duration for which you wish to share your location—be it an hour, until the day's end, or indefinitely.

Upon your sharing of your location, your chosen contact will receive a notification regarding the same. They are then free to opt for sharing their own location in return. Once your contact agrees to share their location with you, you can conveniently track their whereabouts either through a list or on a map, accessible via the Find My app on iPhone, iPad, iPod touch, Mac, or the Find People app on Apple Watch.

If you wish to cease sharing your location with a particular contact, access the Find People screen, tap the name of the contact, and then select "Stop Sharing."

To stop the sharing of your location with everyone, navigate to the Settings app on your Apple Watch. From there, proceed to Privacy & Security > Location Services, and deactivate "Share My Location."

DISCOVER THE WHEREABOUTS OF FRIENDS

Access the Find People app  on your Apple Watch. This will display a list of your friends, each accompanied by their approximate location and the distance from your current position. Employ the Digital Crown to extend your view to more friends.

To pinpoint the exact location of a specific friend on a map, along with an approximate address, tap their name.

When you're ready to return to the list of friends, tap the "<" icon positioned in the top-left corner of the screen.

Alternatively, you can engage Siri by saying, "Where is Julie?"

NOTIFY A FRIEND ABOUT YOUR MOVEMENTS

1. Launch the Find People app on your Apple Watch.
2. Choose the friend you wish to notify, scroll down, and tap "Notify [name of friend]."
3. Activate "Notify [name of friend]" on the following screen. You will then be prompted to decide whether you want to notify your friend when you depart from your location or when you arrive at their location.

RECEIVE NOTIFICATIONS ABOUT YOUR FRIEND'S LOCATION

1. Open the Find People app on your Apple Watch.
2. Select the friend of interest, scroll down, and tap "Notify Me."
3. Turn on "Notify Me," and then make the choice to receive notifications when your friend leaves their current location or when they reach your specified location.

MONITOR YOUR HEART RATE USING APPLE WATCH

Checking your heart rate offers valuable insights into your overall well-being. Apple Watch provides various ways to keep track of your heart rate, whether during workouts, daily activities, Breathe sessions, or whenever you wish.

Note: Ensure both your wrist and Apple Watch are dry and clean to avoid inaccurate readings due to water and sweat.

VIEW YOUR HEART RATE

To observe your current heart rate, resting rate, and walking average rate, access the Heart Rate app on your Apple Watch.

CONTINUAL MONITORING

Your Apple Watch consistently measures your heart rate as long as you are wearing it.

Review Heart Rate Trends

Launch the Heart Rate app 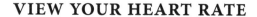 on your Apple Watch.
Tap on "Current," "Resting Heart Rate," or "Walking Average" to display your heart rate data across the day.

For a broader perspective on your heart rate data over a longer timeframe, open the Health app on your iPhone. Navigate to "Browse," tap on "Heart," and choose the desired time frame—hour, day, week, month, or year.

Activate Heart Rate Monitoring

By default, Apple Watch tracks your heart rate during various activities like using the Heart Rate app, workouts, Breathe sessions, and Reflect sessions. If you have previously disabled heart rate tracking, you can enable it again.
1. Access the Settings app on your Apple Watch.
2. Go to "Privacy & Security" and tap on "Health."
3. Select "Heart Rate" and toggle on "Heart Rate."

You can also do this by opening the Apple Watch app on your iPhone, selecting "My Watch," tapping on "Privacy," and then enabling "Heart Rate."

Please remember: For functions such as wrist detection, haptic notifications, blood oxygen level readings (exclusive to Apple Watch Series 6, Apple Watch Series 7, and Apple Watch Series 8), and heart rate monitoring, your Apple Watch's back needs to be in contact with your skin. A comfortable fit—neither too tight nor too loose—ensures optimal functionality while keeping you at ease.

HEART HEALTH WITH APPLE WATCH

Your Apple Watch can serve as a vigilant guardian for your heart health, notifying you of any irregularities. Here are some ways it can keep you informed:

Heart Rate Notifications

Your Apple Watch can send alerts if your heart rate stays above or below a chosen threshold after you've been inactive for at least 10 minutes. You can activate these notifications when you first open the Heart Rate app or later.

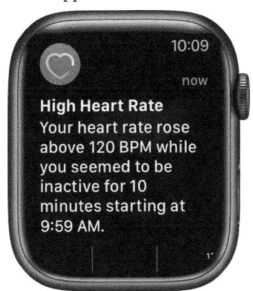

Irregular Heart Rhythm Notifications:
For regions where available, your watch can notify you if it detects an irregular heart rhythm that may indicate atrial fibrillation (AFib). If you've already been diagnosed with AFib, the watch can help you track your heart's arrhythmia frequency and monitor lifestyle factors that influence it.

Enable Notifications
- High or Low Heart Rate Notifications:
  - - Access Settings on your Apple Watch, tap on "Heart," then set a heart rate threshold.
  - - Alternatively, use the Apple Watch app on your iPhone, navigate to My Watch >

Heart, and set the threshold.

Irregular Heart Rhythm Notifications
- Open Settings on your Apple Watch, tap "Heart," and turn on Irregular Rhythm Notifications.
- Or, on your iPhone's Apple Watch app, go to My Watch > Heart and activate Irregular Rhythm.

AFib History Display

For people who live with AFib, the Health app on your iPhone can provide a history of your AFib occurrences. You'll receive weekly notifications estimating the time spent in AFib during the previous calendar week if you've worn your watch adequately.

Cardio Fitness Notifications

Your Apple Watch can estimate your cardio fitness based on heart rate data during outdoor activities. It sends notifications if your cardio fitness level falls into the "Low" range, and every four months thereafter if it remains low.

Enable Notifications

Cardio Fitness Notifications

- In Settings on your Apple Watch, tap "Heart," then activate Cardio Fitness Notifications.

Alternatively, use the Apple Watch app on your iPhone, navigate to My Watch > Heart, and enable Cardio Fitness Notifications.

HOME

Your Apple Watch empowers you to control your smart home efficiently through the Home app. This app lets you command HomeKit-enabled accessories, including lights, locks, thermostats, and more, all with enhanced security. You can also make use of Intercom messages on supported devices and view video streams from HomeKit Secure Video cameras. With your Apple Watch, your home controls are conveniently accessible on your wrist.

GETTING STARTED

1. Set up your home using the Home app  on your iPhone.
2. Define rooms, add HomeKit-enabled accessories, and create scenes.

Accessories, scenes, and rooms added on your iPhone are automatically available on your Apple Watch.

VIEWING HOME STATUS

The Home app on your Apple Watch displays the current status of accessories you're using. For example, you can see the temperature from your thermostat or whether your front door is locked. Simply tap a button to control the accessory or access more details.

CONTROLLING ACCESSORIES AND SCENES

1. Open the Home app  on your Apple Watch.
2. At the top of the screen, you'll find relevant scenes and accessories for that moment.
3. To control an accessory or scene, tap ⚫.

- For accessories like lights, tap ⚫ to turn on/off or adjust settings.
- Swipe left to access additional controls, like brightness or color adjustments.
- To control favorites or accessories in a room, tap the favourites or room, then tap an accessory or tap ⚫ to adjust the settings.
- To view a camera's video stream, tap Cameras and select a camera.

RUNNING SCENES

You can activate pre-defined scenes by opening the Home app on your Apple Watch and tapping the desired scene.

MANAGING MULTIPLE HOMES

- If you have multiple homes set up, you can switch between them on your Apple Watch.
- Open the Home app 🏠 on your Apple Watch.
- If the Home Screen is displayed, tap a home.
- If a specific home is visible, tap "<" and then select a different home.

*Note: T*he Home app allows seamless control of your smart home, including managing HomeKit-enabled accessories and scenes, right from your Apple Watch.

MAIL

Stay on top of your emails with the convenience of your Apple Watch. You can read and respond to messages using various methods, making communication seamless.

READ MAIL NOTIFICATIONS

- When a new mail arrives, just raise your wrist to read the notification.
- Swipe down from the top or tap "Dismiss" to clear the notification.
- If you miss a notification, swipe down on the watch face later to see unread notifications.
- Manage email notifications by going to the Apple Watch app on your iPhone, then navigating to Mail > Custom.

READ MAIL IN THE MAIL APP

1. Open the Mail app  on your Apple Watch.
2. Use the Digital Crown to scroll through the message list.
3. Tap a message to read it.
4. To jump to the top of a lengthy message, turn the Digital Crown or tap the top of the screen.

Messages are formatted for Apple Watch viewing, maintaining most text styles. Tap website links in Mail to view web-formatted content optimized for Apple Watch. Double-tap to zoom in on content.

Note: Website links may not be available in all regions.

SWITCH TO IPHONE

To read a message on your iPhone
1. Wake your iPhone.
2. On iPhones with Face ID, swipe up and pause to open the App Switcher. (On iPhones with a Home button, double-click the Home button to access the App Switcher.)
3. Tap the bottom button to open the Mail app.

COMPOSE AND REPLY TO MAIL

Create a Message:
1. Open the Mail app  on your Apple Watch.
2. Use the Digital Crown to scroll to the top and tap "New Message."
3. Add a recipient by tapping "Add Contact," select the account to send from by tapping "From," create a subject by tapping "Add Subject," and then tap "Create Message."
• If you've set up multiple languages, tap "Language," choose a language, then tap the "Create Message" field.

COMPOSE AND REPLY METHODS

• Reply using the QWERTY and QuickPath keyboard (Apple Watch Series 7 and 8, select languages).
• Use dictation 🎤, Scribble ✍️, emoji 😃, or prepared responses.
• If needed, switch to your iPhone to type a response.

REPLY TO A MESSAGE IN THE MAIL APP

1. Open the Mail app ✉️ on your Apple Watch.
2. Scroll to the bottom of the message you want to reply to.
3. Tap "Reply."
   • If there are multiple recipients, tap "Reply All."
   • Tap "Add Message," and then proceed with the following methods to reply on the next page.

SMART REPLIES

1. To send a smart reply, scroll to view a list of useful phrases. Simply tap one to send it.
2. Customize smart replies by opening the Apple Watch app on your iPhone.
3. Navigate to My Watch > Mail > Default Replies > Add reply.
4. Reorder or delete default replies by tapping "Edit" and dragging or tapping the delete icon ⊖.
5. If the available smart replies aren't in the language you need, scroll down, tap "Languages," and choose a language.

Note: The available languages are those enabled on your iPhone via Settings > General > Keyboard > Keyboards.

COMPOSE YOUR OWN REPLY

- Tap the "Add Message" field to compose a personalized reply.

REPLY ON IPHONE

1. If you prefer to respond on your iPhone:
2. Wake your iPhone and open the App Switcher.
    - On iPhones with Face ID, swipe up from the bottom edge and pause.
    - On iPhones with a Home button, double-click the Home button.

3. Tap the button at the bottom of the screen to open the email in the Mail app on your iPhone.

MAPS

Discover and Navigate with Ease Using Apple Watch's Maps App

Your Apple Watch is equipped with a Maps app  that lets you explore your surroundings and find your way with ease.

DISCOVER PLACES WITH SIRI

- Use Siri for quick queries like:
- "Where am I?"
- "Find coffee near me."

SEARCH ON THE MAP

1. Open the Maps app on your Apple Watch.
2. Tap "Search," then use voice dictation, scribble, or the QWERTY and QuickPath keyboard (available on Apple Watch Series 7 and Series 8, and not in all languages).
3. On Apple Watch Series 7 and Series 8, access Scribble by swiping up from the bottom of the screen and tapping "Scribble."

FIND NEARBY SERVICES

1. Open the Maps app on your Apple Watch.
2. Tap the ☰, then select a category like Restaurants or Parking.
3. Choose a result to view details, and scroll using the Digital Crown.
4. Tap "<" in the top-left corner to go back to the list of results.

EXPLORE GUIDES

1. Open the Maps app on your iPhone.
2. Tap the search field, swipe up, and:
   - Tap a cover below City Guides or Guides We Love.
   - Tap "Explore Guides" to browse and tap a guide cover.
   - Tap an entry below Browse by Publisher, then tap a cover.
3. Swipe up, tap ✛ next to a location's name, and choose a guide or tap "New Guide."
4. On your Apple Watch, scroll down and tap the guide to view its locations.

VIEW AND SEARCH YOUR CURRENT LOCATION

1. Open the Maps app  on your Apple Watch.
2. Tap "Location" to see your current location.
3. To search around your location, tap the magnifying glass icon and tap • • • "Search Here."
   - Tap "Transit Map" to view nearby transit options.

INTERACT WITH THE MAP

- Pan the map: Drag with one finger.
- Zoom in or out: Turn the Digital Crown.
- Double-tap to zoom in on a location.
- Return to your current location: Tap ⌁ at the bottom right.

PLAN ROUTES AND GET DIRECTIONS

- Open the Maps app  on your Apple Watch.
- Scroll to Favorites, Guides, or Recents, and tap an entry for directions.
- Select a mode for driving, walking, transit, or cycling directions.
- Choose an alternate route, adjust preferences, and see route details.
- Tap a route to start navigation and see an overview with turns and distances.

EXPLORING LANDMARKS AND MARKED LOCATIONS

1. Tap the marker on the map for the chosen spot.
2. Use the Digital Crown to view details.
3. Tap "<" at the top left to go back to the map.

*Note: T*o call the location, tap its phone number. For iPhone access, use the App Switcher. (Swipe up from the bottom edge for Face ID iPhones or double-click the Home button for iPhones with a Home button.) Tap the button at the screen's bottom to open Phone.

PLACING, ADJUSTING, AND REMOVING PINS

- Place a pin: Press and hold on the map, wait for the pin to drop, then release.
  - To drop a pin at your current spot, tap the blue dot, then "Mark My Location."
- Adjust a pin: Press and hold to move it or place a new pin.
- Remove a pin: Tap it, see address info, scroll with the Digital Crown, then tap "Remove Marker."

ACCESSING RECENT LOCATIONS

1. Open Maps app  on your Apple Watch.
2. Scroll down, tap a location under "Recents."
   - "Recents" may include recently viewed guides from your iPhone.

GETTING DIRECTIONS

ASK SIRI

- "Directions to the nearest gas station?"
- "Get directions home."
- "How far to the airport?"

Note: Drop a pin on the map to estimate an address, then tap the pin to view address info.

FETCHING DIRECTIONS

1. Launch the Maps app on your Apple Watch.
2. Scroll to Favorites, Guides, or Recents.
3. Tap an entry for driving, walking, transit, or cycling directions.
4. Choose a mode, see suggested routes, and tap a route for an overview.
   - Find your estimated arrival time at the top left. Tap it to check arrival time.

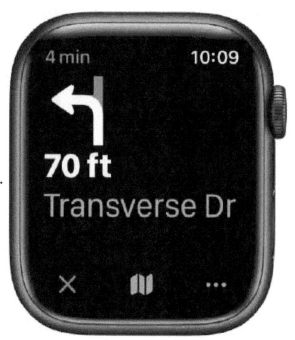

Note: When selecting Cycling, see elevation changes on the route overview. Tap ● ● ● to learn about road types—bike paths, main roads, or walking-required roads.

MEDICATIONS

Take charge of your medications, vitamins, and supplements through the Health app on your iPhone. The Medications app 💊 on your Apple Watch allows you to monitor and log your medications, along with setting up reminders.

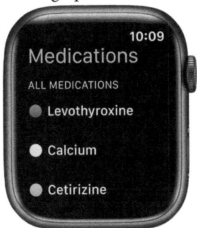

Note: The Medications feature should never replace professional medical advice. While additional info might be on your medication labels, it's vital to consult your healthcare provider before making any health-related choices.

CREATING A MEDICATION SCHEDULE ON IPHONE

1. Launch the Health app on your iPhone, tap Browse at the bottom right, and then tap Medications.
2. Choose to Add Medication (if you're starting your list) or Add a Medication (if you're adding more).
3. Identify your medication using these options:

Type the name: Tap the search field, type the name, and tap Add.

- For U.S. users, suggestions appear while you type, and you can pick one or finish typing and add.

Use the camera Option 📷
Tap next to the search field and follow onscreen instructions.
If there's no match, tap Search by Name, then type it as above.

Follow onscreen instructions to create a visual identifier, set a schedule, and understand potential interactions.

LOGGING YOUR MEDICATIONS

Your Apple Watch reminds you to take medications as per your schedule in the Health app 🖤 on iPhone.

Follow these steps to log them:
1. Tap a notification if it prompts you to log your medications, or open the Medications app on your Apple Watch.
2. Tap the current medication schedule, e.g., morning medications.
3. Tap Log All as Taken.
   - This records dosage, units taken, and the time. To log individual medications, scroll down, tap a medication under Your Medications, and then tap Log.
   - The medication name and time logged will be visible under Logged.

To update a logged medication, tap it, select Taken or Skipped, and then tap Done.

You can view your log and medication history on your iPhone's Health app under Browse and Medications.

MEMOJI

Unleash your creativity with the Memoji app 🧑, where you can craft your own unique Memoji persona. Customize features like skin tone, freckles, hairstyle, facial traits, glasses, headwear, and more. Multiple Memojis can be designed to reflect various moods.

CRAFTING A MEMOJI

1. Open the Memoji app 🧑 on your Apple Watch.
2. If it's your first time using the Memoji app, tap Get Started.
   - If you've previously made a Memoji, scroll down, and tap ⊕ to create a new one.
3. Tap each feature and use the Digital Crown to select your desired options. Watch your Memoji come to life as you add details like hairstyle and eyewear.
4. Tap Done to add your new Memoji to the collection.
5. The Memojis you create can be used as stickers in Messages.

For another Memoji, tap ⊕ and then add features.

EDITING MEMOJI AND MORE

Open the Memoji app 🧑 on your Apple Watch, tap a Memoji, and explore these options

- Edit a Memoji: Tap features like eyes and headwear, then turn the Digital Crown to choose a variation.
- Craft a Memoji watch face: Scroll down and tap Create Watch Face.
  Swipe left on your watch face to discover your new Memoji watch face. This face is also included in your watch face collection on the Apple Watch app on your iPhone.
- Duplicate a Memoji: Scroll down and tap Duplicate.
- Delete a Memoji: Scroll down and tap Delete.

MESSAGES

Stay connected by reading incoming text messages directly on your Apple Watch. Respond using the QWERTY and QuickPath keyboard (only available on Apple Watch Series 7 and Apple Watch Series 8 in certain languages), dictation, Scribble, prepared responses, or switch to your iPhone for longer replies.

STEPS TO READ A MESSAGE

1. Feel a tap or hear an alert sound indicating a new message? Raise your Apple Watch to read it.
2. Turn the Digital Crown to scroll through the message content.
3. Tap the top of the screen to swiftly navigate to the message's beginning.

Note: Web links within messages are tappable for viewing web-formatted content, and double-tap to zoom in. If the message is from a while ago, touch and hold the top of the screen, swipe down to see the message notification, then tap to read. To mark the message as read, scroll down and tap Dismiss. To dismiss the notification without marking it as read, press the Digital Crown.

DETERMINING SENT TIMES

To check when messages were sent, swipe left on a message within a conversation in the Messages conversation list.

MUTING OR DELETING CONVERSATIONS

- Mute a conversation: Swipe left on a conversation in the Messages conversation list and tap 🔕.
- Delete a conversation: Swipe left on a conversation in the Messages conversation list and tap 🗑.

ACCESSING PHOTOS, AUDIO, MUSIC, AND VIDEO

Messages can include multimedia content. Follow these steps to access them on your Apple Watch

- Photo: Tap a photo to view, double-tap to enlarge, and drag to navigate. Tap < in the top-left corner to return. To share, tap the photo, then select the sharing option ⬆. To save it, scroll down and tap Save Image or Create Watch Face.

- Audio Clip: Tap the clip to listen. Tap Keep to retain it for longer. It remains for 30 days, but you can adjust this on your iPhone's settings.
- Music: Tap a song, album, or playlist to play it in the Music app (Apple Music subscription required).
- Video: Tap a video to play it fullscreen. Control playback with taps and swipes. Save videos by opening the message on your iPhone.

MANAGING MESSAGE NOTIFICATIONS

1. Open the Apple Watch app on your iPhone.
2. Tap My Watch, then Messages.
3. Customize notification options under Custom to determine how you're notified when receiving messages.

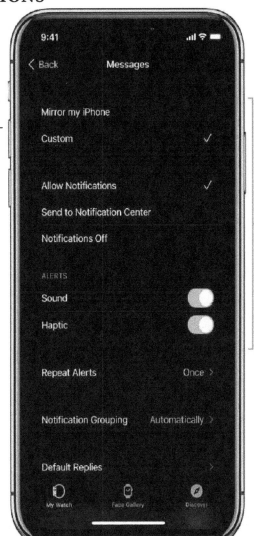

Note that certain Focus settings might affect message notifications.

SENDING MESSAGES FROM YOUR APPLE WATCH

Stay in touch effortlessly by composing and sending messages from your Apple Watch. Not only can you include text, but you can also add images, emoji 😊, Memoji stickers 🐵, audio clips 🎤, and even send money through Apple Pay 🍎Cash or share your location.

CREATING A MESSAGE

1. Launch the Messages app on your Apple Watch.
2. Scroll to the top and tap New Message.
3. Add a contact by tapping Add Contact or selecting from recent conversations. Alternatively, you can:
   - Use the search field or dictate a phone number 🎤 .
   - Choose from your entire list of contacts 👤 .
   - Manually enter a phone number ⊞ .
4. Tap Create Message.
5. If you use multiple languages on your Apple Watch, select a language if needed.

COMPOSING A TEXT MESSAGE

Composing a message is simple. After creating a message, tap the Create Message field and use any of the following methods to compose your message:

- Utilize Scribble: Write your message with your finger. Edit using the Digital Crown and use predictive text.
- Dictate text: Tap the microphone icon 🎤 , speak your message, and tap Done. Punctuation can also be dictated.
- Use the QWERTY and QuickPath keyboard: (Available on Apple Watch Series 7 and Apple Watch Series 8, but not in all languages) Enter characters or swipe with Quick-Path to form words.
- Include emoji 😀: Access frequently used or browse categories to find the right emoji.
- Use your iPhone keyboard: If your paired iPhone is nearby, you can use its keyboard to compose messages.

SENDING VARIOUS TYPES OF MESSAGES FROM YOUR APPLE WATCH

Diversify your messaging style by choosing from a range of options without needing to type a single character. Once you've created your message, explore these alternatives:

SMART REPLY

Swipe to view a collection of convenient phrases that you can use. Tap one to select, then tap Send.

To customize these options, go to the Apple Watch app on your iPhone, select My Watch, navigate to Messages > Default Replies, and tap Add Reply. For further personalization, you can tap Edit to reorder or delete phrases by tappying ⊖ .

If the smart replies are not in your desired language, scroll down, select Languages, and choose the appropriate language. These languages align with those enabled on your iPhone under Settings > General > Keyboard > Keyboards.

MEMOJI STICKER

Tap ⬆️, navigate through the Memoji Stickers collection, choose a variation, and then tap 🖼️ Send.

STICKER

Tap ⬆️, tap 😀, scroll to the bottom, and then tap More Stickers. Select a sticker and tap Send. For creating new stickers or viewing your full collection, utilize the Messages app on your iPhone.

GIF

Tap ⬆️, tap 🔍, select a GIF, and then tap Send. If you need a specific GIF, enter a search term in the Search field, tap a resulting GIF, and then tap Send.

AUDIO CLIP

Tap ⬆️, tap 🎙️, record your mess age, tap Done, and then tap Send.

USING APPLE CASH FOR TRANSACTIONS

1. While in a conversation, tap ⬆️ next to the iMessage field.
2. Tap 💵Cash.
3. Adjust the amount using the Digital Crown, then tap Send.
4. Double-click the side button to send the payment.

Note: Availability of Apple Cash varies by region.

SHARE YOUR LOCATION

To send someone a map showing your current location, scroll down, then tap Send Location.

On your paired iPhone, make sure Share My Location is turned on in Settings ⚙ > [your name] > Find My > Share My Location. Or, on your Apple Watch with cellular, open the Settings app , go to Privacy > Location Services, then turn on Share My Location.

Messages screen showing a map of the sender's location.

— Share your location in a message.

CONTACT THE PERSON YOU'RE MESSAGING

1. While viewing a conversation, scroll down.
2. Tap Details, then tap 📞 , 📞 , ✉ , or ⬤ .

Scroll down and tap Share Contact to share the contact with others.

RESPONDING TO MESSAGES ON YOUR APPLE WATCH

Replying to a Message

Scroll down using the Digital Crown to reach the bottom of the message, and then select your preferred method of reply.

You can also use Tapbacks for quick responses—press and hold a specific message in the conversation, then choose a Tapback option like thumbs-up or heart.

Direct Reply to a Specific Message

In a group conversation, you can provide a direct response to a particular message to maintain organized conversations.

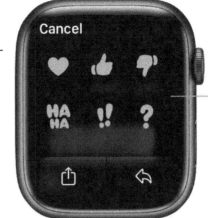

1. Within a Messages conversation, hold your finger on a specific message you wish to reply to.
2. Tap ↩.
3. Craft your response and tap Send.
   The message you send will only be visible to the recipient of your response.

Double-tap a message, then tap to choose a Tapback.

Sharing Messages with Others

1. In a Messages conversation, touch and hold a specific message Tap ⬆.
2. Choose recipients you frequently exchange messages with, or select Messages or Mail.
3. If you opt for Messages or Mail, add contacts and include a subject if sending an email.
4. Tap Send.

MINDFULNESS

Utilize your Apple Watch to embrace mindfulness through the Mindfulness app 🌀. This app encourages you to allocate a few minutes each day for focusing, centering, and connecting with your breath. Additionally, with an Apple Fitness+ subscription, you can access guided meditations directly on your Apple Watch.

STARTING A REFLECT OR BREATHE SESSION

Begin your mindfulness journey by opening the Mindfulness app 🌀 on your Apple Watch, and then follow these steps:

- For Reflect: Tap Reflect, read the theme, concentrate your attention, and tap Begin.
- For Breathe: Tap Breathe, slowly inhale as the animation expands, and exhale as it contracts.

To conclude a session before its completion, swipe to the right and tap End.

ADJUSTING SESSION DURATION

Customize your mindfulness experience by setting the session duration:

1. Open the Mindfulness app on your Apple Watch.

2. Tap , choose Duration, and then select a duration from one to five minutes.

FINE-TUNING MINDFULNESS SETTINGS

Tailor your mindfulness practice with these setting adjustments:
1. Open the Settings app ⚙ on your Apple Watch.
2. Tap Mindfulness, and then make the following adjustments
   - Reminders: Turn Start of Day and End of Day reminders on or off; add extra reminders as needed.
   - Weekly Summary: Toggle Weekly Summary on or off.
   - Mute Reminders: Activate "Mute for today."
   - Breath Rate: Adjust the breaths per minute by tapping Breath Rate.
   - Haptics Settings: Tap Haptics, and choose None, Minimal, or Prominent.
   - New Meditations: Enable Add New Meditations to Watch to download fresh meditations when your watch is charging. Completed meditations are automatically removed.

You can also adjust these settings via the Apple Watch app on your iPhone by navigating to My Watch > Mindfulness.

MONITORING HEART RATE DURING SESSIONS

After completing a Reflect or Breathe session, your heart rate is displayed on the Summary screen. For a more detailed review, access your heart rate information later by launching the Health app on your iPhone, tapping Browse, then Heart > Heart Rate. Swipe up and tap Breathe.

USING THE BREATHE WATCH FACE

Quickly access mindfulness sessions by adding the Breathe watch face:

1. On your current watch face, press and hold the display.
2. Swipe left until you reach the end, then tap the New button (+).
3. Rotate the Digital Crown to select Breathe, and tap Add.
4. Tap the watch face to open the Mindfulness app.

SUBSCRIPTION MINDFULNESS

Enjoy Guided Meditations with Your Apple Watch

If you're an Apple Fitness+ subscriber, you can indulge in guided meditations through your Apple Watch while it's paired with AirPods, Bluetooth headphones, or speakers. Please note that Apple Fitness+ availability varies by country and region.

STARTING A GUIDED MEDITATION

To begin your soothing meditation experience, follow these straightforward steps

1. Launch the Mindfulness app on your Apple Watch.
2. Tap Fitness+ Audio Meditations.
3. Scroll through the meditation options to find one that resonates with you.
   - Details like the theme, trainer, and duration of the meditation are displayed towards the bottom of each episode.
4. Tap (i) to access more information about the meditation, add it to your library, or play its playlist in the Music app.
5. Choose a meditation to initiate the session.
   - During the meditation, Apple Watch will show the elapsed time and your current heart rate.

To pause or conclude a guided meditation, swipe right while the meditation is playing, then tap Pause or End. If you wish to start a workout while continuing with the meditation, tap Workout and select a suitable workout.

REVIEWING COMPLETED MEDITATIONS

1. Once you've finished a meditation, it's stored in My Library. To access this collection, you can use your Apple Watch or the Fitness app on your iPhone.
2. Open the Mindfulness app on your Apple Watch.
3. Tap Fitness+ Audio Meditations.
   - Scroll to the bottom of the screen and tap My Library to view the meditations you've enjoyed.
4. Tap (i) to gather more insights about a meditation, download it, remove it from your library, or play its playlist in the Music app.

Opt for a meditation to replay it whenever you like.

You can also explore your library across your iPhone, iPad, or Apple TV. Just open the Fitness app on your device (access Fitness+ on iPhone) and navigate to My Library.

MUSIC

Manage Your Music Collection on Apple Watch

ADD MUSIC TO APPLE WATCH

By adding music to your Apple Watch, you ensure that you can enjoy your favorite tunes wherever you are, even without your iPhone by your side. Here's how you can do it.

USING YOUR IPHONE

- Open the Apple Watch app 🎵 on your iPhone.
- Tap "My Watch" and then select "Music."
- Under "Playlists & Albums," tap "Add Music."
- Choose the specific albums and playlists you'd like to sync with your Apple Watch.

USING YOUR APPLE WATCH

- If you're an Apple Music subscriber, you can directly add music using your Apple Watch.
- Open the Music app 🎵 on your watch.
- Tap "Listen Now" or "Search" and navigate to the music you want to add.
- Select a playlist or album, then tap ••• the "Add to Library" option.
- A confirmation message will let you know the item has been added.

Keep in mind that music you've recently listened to will automatically be added if you're an Apple Music subscriber. If you haven't played anything, Apple Music's recommendations will be added.

ADD A WORKOUT PLAYLIST

For those workout sessions, you can set up a playlist that plays automatically when you start a workout using the Workout app on your Apple Watch. Here's how:

USING YOUR IPHONE

- Open the Apple Watch app 🎵 on your iPhone.
- Tap "My Watch," then select "Workout."
- Under "Workout Playlist," choose a playlist to associate with your workouts.

REMOVE MUSIC FROM APPLE WATCH

If you need to free up space or simply want to tidy up your music collection on your Apple Watch, you can remove music as needed:

USING YOUR IPHONE

- Open the Apple Watch app 🎵 on your iPhone.
- Tap "My Watch," then select "Music."
- For music you've added, tap Edit, then tap ➖ to reove the items you want.
- To remove automatically added music, toggle off "Recent Music" or other auto-added options.

USING YOUR APPLE WATCH

- If you're an Apple Music subscriber, you can remove music directly from your watch.
- Open the Music app 🎵 on your watch.
- Navigate to "Library," then "Downloaded," and select "Playlists" or "Albums."
- Swipe left on a playlist or album, tap ••• then tap Remove, then confirm by tapping "Delete."

Remember that songs or playlists removed from your Apple Watch will also be removed from other devices using the same Apple ID. To check how much music is stored on your Apple Watch, go to settings ⚙️ > "General" > "Storage" on your watch or "General" > "Storage" in the Apple Watch app on your iPhone.

PLAYING MUSIC ON YOUR APPLE WATCH

The Music app 🎵 on your Apple Watch lets you easily choose and play music. Whether you want to listen to songs stored on your watch, control music on your iPhone, or stream from Apple Music or Apple Music Voice (subscription required), you can do it all. Here's how.

USING SIRI

You can ask Siri to play specific songs, albums, or playlists for you. Just say things like:

- "Play 'enough for you' by Olivia Rodrigo."
- "Play more songs from this album."
- "Play my workout playlist."
- "Play Apple Music Country."
- "Play cool jazz."
- "Play the dinner party playlist."
- "Play a playlist to help me relax."
- "Play more like this."

PLAYING MUSIC

Once your Apple Watch is connected to Bluetooth headphones or speakers, follow these steps to play music using the Music app :

PLAY MUSIC ON APPLE WATCH

- Open the Music app on your Apple Watch.
- Turn the Digital Crown to browse through album artwork.
- Tap a playlist or album to start playing it.
- Use the Apple Watch app on your iPhone to manage which songs are available on your Apple Watch.

PLAY MUSIC FROM YOUR IPHONE (NO BLUETOOTH PAIRING REQUIRED)

- Scroll to the top of the screen on your Apple Watch.
- Tap "On iPhone."
- Select a playlist, artist, album, or song to play from your iPhone's music library.

PLAY MUSIC FROM YOUR MUSIC LIBRARY

- Open the Music app on your Apple Watch.
- Tap "Library."
- Choose a playlist, artist, album, or song to play.
- For music already downloaded to your watch, tap "Downloaded" and select the music.

REQUEST MUSIC FROM APPLE MUSIC

- If you're an Apple Music or Apple Music Voice subscriber, you can ask for specific music by raising your wrist.
- Request an artist, album, song, genre, or part of a song lyric.

PERSONALIZED MUSIC

As an Apple Music subscriber, you can enjoy music personalized for you:

1. Open the Music app  on your Apple Watch.
2. Scroll to the top and tap "Listen Now."
3. Explore playlists and albums curated based on your preferences.
4. Tap a category, then an album or playlist, and tap the play button ▶.

Tap for more options.

MANAGING THE QUEUE

When playing music, you can manage the queue of upcoming songs:

1. Open the Music app  on your Apple Watch.
2. Start playing an album or playlist, then tap the queue icon ☰.
3. Tap a track in the queue to play it.

Auto Play adds similar music to the queue's end. To disable Auto Play, tap the ∞ option.

To add songs of your choice to the queue, swipe left on a song, playlist, or album; tap the ••• icon, then select "Play Next" or "Play Last." Remember, turning off Auto Play on one device won't affect other devices using your Apple ID.

CONTROLLING PLAYBACK AND MORE WITH MUSIC ON YOUR APPLE WATCH

ADJUSTING VOLUME

Turn the Digital Crown to control the volume. You can use these controls to manage music playback on both your Apple Watch and iPhone:

- Play the current song.
- Pause playback.

- Skip to the next song.
- Double-tap to skip to the previous song or to return to the beginning of the current song.

▶	Play the current song.
❚❚	Pause playback.
▶▶	Skip to the next song.
◀◀	Skip to the beginning of the song; double-tap to skip to the previous song.

SHUFFLE AND REPEAT

You can shuffle albums, songs, and artists from the Music screen:
- Tap an album, artist, or playlist.
- Tap the shuffle icon ⤬ to shuffle the content.

You can also control shuffle and repeat from the playback screen:
- While music is playing, tap the three dots •••.
- Choose ⤬ or ⟲ to customize your listening experience.
Tap the "Repeat" ⟲ icon twice to repeat a song.

USING MUSIC ON APPLE WATCH

You can interact with your music library on Apple Watch:
- While music is playing, tap the three dots ••• on the Now Playing screen for more options.
- Swipe left on a song, playlist, or album in Listen Now and Library, then tap the ••• icon for more choices.
- Tap ＋ to add items to your library from these options.

SHARING MUSIC

If you're an Apple Music subscriber, you can share playlists, albums, and songs:
1. Open the Music app 🎵 on your Apple Watch.
2. Choose where you want to start (On iPhone, Listen Now, or Library).
3. Tap Playlists, Albums, or Songs.
4. Swipe left on a playlist, album, or song.
5. Tap the ••• icon, then select "Share [Playlist, Album, Song]."
6. Choose a sharing method.
You can also share a song directly from the Now Playing screen by tapping the ••• icon and selecting "Share Song." For songs from radio stations, choose "Share Station."

CELLULAR CONNECTION SETTINGS

To listen to music over cellular, follow these steps:

1. On your iPhone, go to Settings ⚙ > Music.
2. Turn on Cellular Data.
3. Tap Audio Quality > Cellular Streaming, then choose a quality setting. Note that higher quality settings use more data.

LISTENING TO RADIO ON APPLE WATCH

The Music app 🎵 on your Apple Watch offers a variety of radio options, including Apple Music 1, Apple Music Hits, Apple Music Country, and broadcast radio stations:

LISTENING TO APPLE MUSIC RADIO

- Open the Music app 🎵 on your Apple Watch.
- Tap Radio, then select Apple Music 1, Apple Music Hits, or Apple Music Country.

LISTENING TO FEATURED OR GENRE STATIONS

- Open the Music app 🎵 on your Apple Watch.
- Tap Radio, and use the Digital Crown to browse stations and genres crafted by music experts.
- Tap a genre to explore its stations, and select a station to start listening.

LISTENING TO BROADCAST RADIO

You can enjoy broadcast radio stations on your Apple Watch by asking Siri. For example, say "Play Wild 94.9" or "Tune in to ESPN Radio." You can use station names, call signs, frequencies, or nicknames.

Please note that some features may not be available in the Apple Music Voice Plan. For more details, refer to the Apple Support article on Apple Music Voice. Also, broadcast radio availability varies by country or region.

NEWS

Reading News Stories on Your Apple Watch

The News app  on your Apple Watch keeps you informed about current events by presenting news stories tailored to your interests.

WAYS TO ACCESS NEWS STORIES

- Open the News app  directly on your Apple Watch.
- Tap the News complication on a watch face.
- Tap a news item on the Siri watch face.
- Tap a notification from the News app.

READING A NEWS STORY

1. Open the News app  on your Apple Watch.
2. Use the Digital Crown to scroll through the story summary.
3. If you wish to read the full story on your iPhone, iPad, or Mac, scroll to the bottom of the summary and tap "Save for Later."

READING STORIES ON OTHER DEVICES

- iPhone: Open the News app  on your iPhone, tap "Following," then "Saved Stories." Locate and tap the story.
- iPad: Open the News app  on your iPad, tap "Saved Stories" in the sidebar, then select the story.
- Mac: Open the News app  on your Mac, click "Saved Stories" in the sidebar, and click the story.

CUSTOMIZING NEWS FEEDS

To read stories only from the channels you follow, you can restrict stories in Today

1. Open the Settings app ⚙ on your iPhone.
2. Tap "News," then turn on "Restrict Stories in Today."

Please be aware that restricting stories limits the variety of content in Today and other feeds. If you follow only one channel, your feed will consist mainly of stories from that channel. This setting removes Top Stories and Trending Stories.

NAVIGATING NEWS STORIES

1. Open the News app 📰 on your Apple Watch.
2. Swipe left to move to the next available story.
3. Swipe right to return to the previous story.

If you're reading the summary, tap "Next Story" at the bottom to proceed.

OPENING STORIES ON IPHONE

To open news stories on your iPhone from your Apple Watch

1. Open the News app 📰 on your Apple Watch.
2. Wake your iPhone and access the App Switcher (swipe up from the bottom edge or double-click the Home button on iPhones with Face ID).
3. Tap the button that appears at the bottom of the screen to open the News app on your iPhone.

NOISE

Measuring Environmental Noise with Your Apple Watch

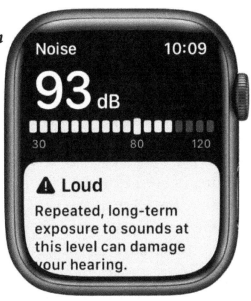

USING THE NOISE APP

The Noise app on your Apple Watch gauges the surrounding sound levels by utilizing the microphone and monitoring duration. It can alert you with a wrist tap when noise reaches a level that could impact your hearing.

Please note that the Noise app employs the microphone solely for measuring sound levels; no sounds are recorded or stored for this purpose.

TO CONFIGURE THE NOISE APP

1. Open the Noise app 🎧 on your Apple Watch.
2. Tap "Enable" to activate monitoring.
3. For future environmental noise measurements, access the Noise app 🎧 or use the Noise complication.

RECEIVING NOISE NOTIFICATIONS

1. Open the Settings app ⚙️ on your Apple Watch.
2. Navigate to Noise > Noise Notifications and select your preferred setting.
You can also adjust this in the Apple Watch app on your iPhone under My Watch > Noise > Noise Threshold.

DISABLING NOISE MEASUREMENT

1. Open the Settings app ⚙️ on your Apple Watch.
2. Go to Noise > Environmental Sound Measurements and switch off "Measure Sounds."
You can also adjust this in the Apple Watch app on your iPhone under My Watch > Noise, then toggle off "Environmental Sound Measurements."

ENVIRONMENTAL NOISE MONITORING

When you pair your Apple Watch with your iPhone and set up the Noise app 👂 on your watch, the data on environmental sound levels is automatically transmitted to the Health app on your iPhone (requires watchOS 6 or later).

VIEWING NOISE NOTIFICATIONS DETAILS

When the noise level around you might impact your hearing, Apple Watch sends notifications to your iPhone.
To view the details:
1. Open the Health app 🤍 on your iPhone.
2. Tap "Summary" at the bottom left.
3. Tap the notification near the top of the screen, then select "Show More Data."

TRACKING EXPOSURE OVER TIME

To observe your exposure to environmental noise levels:
1. Open the Health app 🤍 on your iPhone.
2. Tap "Browse" at the bottom right, then choose "Hearing."
3. Tap "Environmental Sound Levels" and utilize the following options:

- Tabs at the top display exposure levels over different periods.
- Tap the information icon (i) to learn about sound level classifications.
- Swipe the graph to adjust the displayed time span.
- Touch and hold the graph to view details about a specific moment.
- Tap "Show More Data" for average exposure details.
- Tap "Exposure" below the graph to see a line indicating average exposure.
- Tap "Show More Data," then "Range" to view the high and low range of noise levels.

PHONE

CONTROL AUDIO PLAYBACK

Now Playing empowers you to manage audio playback on Apple Watch, iPhone, and other connected devices.

ACCESS NOW PLAYING

You can access Now Playing through various methods
- Open the Now Playing app ▶ on your Apple Watch.
- Press the side button and tap "Now Playing" in the Dock (it's the first item).
- Tap the Now Playing complication if you've added it to your watch face.

CONTROL MUSIC, PODCASTS, OR AUDIOBOOKS ON IPHONE

1. Launch the Music 🎵, Podcasts 🎙, or audiobook 📖 app on your iPhone and begin playing a song, podcast, or audiobook.
2. Open Now Playing ▶ on your Apple Watch to utilize controls like play, pause, and more.
3. Use the Digital Crown to adjust the volume.

USING NOW PLAYING WITH DIFFERENT DEVICES

If multiple devices can play audio, such as an Apple Watch, iPhone, and HomePod

- The top-left corner displays the name of the device you're currently controlling.
- Tap "<" to reveal a list of available devices and choose one to control it.

PHONE

ANSWER A CALL

- Lift your wrist to view the caller's information.
- To send the call to voicemail, tap the red "Decline" button.
- To answer on your Apple Watch, tap "Answer" and utilize the built-in microphone and speaker or a paired Bluetooth device.
- If you prefer to answer with your iPhone or send a text message instead, tap ••• and choose an option.
- If you select "Answer on iPhone," the call is put on hold, and the caller hears a repeated sound until you answer on your iPhone.

  If you can't find your iPhone, touch and hold the ••• bottom of the screen, swipe up, then tap (( )) on your Apple Watch.

DURING THE CALL

- Switch the call from your Apple Watch to your iPhone by unlocking your iPhone and tapping the green button or bar.
- Adjust the call volume by turning the Digital Crown. You can also tap 🎤 to mute your end of the call.
- Enter digits using the keypad if needed by tapping ● ● ● , then selecting "Keypad."
- Switch the call's audio to another device by tapping ● ● ● , then choosing a device.
- During a FaceTime Audio call, adjust the volume, mute the call with 🎤 , or choose an audio destination.

LISTENING TO VOICEMAIL

If you receive voicemail, you'll get a notification. Tap the Play button to listen to it. You can also listen later by opening the Phone app 📞 on your Apple Watch and tapping "Voicemail."

ON THE VOICEMAIL SCREEN, YOU CAN:

- Adjust volume using the Digital Crown.
- Start and stop playback.
- Skip ahead or back five seconds.
- Call back the voicemail sender.
- Delete the voicemail.

MAKING PHONE CALLS

You can easily make phone calls using voice commands or manually.

- Ask Siri to call someone or dial a specific number.
- Open the Phone app 📞 on your Apple Watch, tap "Contacts," choose a contact, and tap the phone button.
- Dial a number directly by tapping "Keypad," entering the number, and tapping .
- For recent contacts or favorites, tap "Recents" or "Favorites" respectively.

MAKING CALLS OVER WI-FI ON APPLE WATCH

If your cellular provider supports Wi-Fi calling, you can use your Apple Watch to make and receive calls over Wi-Fi instead of relying on the cellular network. This is particularly useful when your paired iPhone isn't accessible or powered off. Your Apple Watch must be within range of a Wi-Fi network that your iPhone has previously connected to.

SETTING UP WI-FI CALLING

1. On your iPhone, navigate to Settings ⚙ > Phone.
2. Tap "Wi-Fi Calling" and enable both "Wi-Fi Calling on This iPhone" and "Add Wi-Fi Calling for Other Devices."
3. Open the Phone app 📞 on your Apple Watch.
4. Choose a contact and tap 📞.
5. Select the desired phone number or FaceTime address for the call.

IMPORTANT NOTE ON EMERGENCY CALLS

While you can make emergency calls over Wi-Fi, it's recommended to use your iPhone over a cellular connection whenever possible for more accurate location information. If needed, you can temporarily disconnect your Apple Watch from Wi-Fi to ensure you're using your iPhone for emergency calls.

VIEWING CALL INFORMATION ON APPLE WATCH

While engaged in a call on your iPhone, you can access call details on your Apple Watch using the Phone app 📞. You can also end the call from your Apple Watch, especially useful when you're using earphones or a headset.

USING DUAL SIM IPHONE WITH APPLE WATCH

If you have a Dual SIM iPhone with multiple cellular plans, you can also use multiple lines on your Apple Watch with cellular capabilities. Here's how:

1. Set up your first plan during initial watch setup.
2. To add a second plan, open the Apple Watch app on your iPhone, go to My Watch > Cellular > Set Up Cellular or Add a New Plan.
3. Follow the steps to select the additional plan for your Apple Watch.

SWITCHING BETWEEN PLANS

1. On your Apple Watch, navigate to Settings ⚙ > Cellular.
2. Choose the desired plan for your watch to use.

RECEIVING CALLS AND MESSAGES WITH MULTIPLE PLANS

- When your Apple Watch is connected to your iPhone, you can receive calls and messages from both plans. The watch indicates which line received the notification.
- If your Apple Watch is connected to cellular and your iPhone isn't nearby, calls and messages come through based on the line you've chosen in the Apple Watch app.

PHOTOS

Managing Photos on Apple Watch

CHOOSING PHOTO ALBUMS AND STORAGE

The Photos app  on your Apple Watch enables you to enjoy photos from your chosen iPhone album, highlighted photos, and Memories.

SELECTING THE ALBUM TO DISPLAY

Initially, your Apple Watch showcases photos from your Favorites album—pictures you've marked as favorites. However, you can modify this setting.

1. Open the Apple Watch app on your iPhone.
2. Navigate to My Watch > Photos > Sync Album, and then select your preferred album.

REMOVING PHOTOS FROM APPLE WATCH

To delete a photo from your Apple Watch, access the Photos app on your iPhone, and delete the picture from the synced album.

DISPLAYING FEATURED PHOTOS AND MEMORIES

Your Apple Watch can automatically sync featured photos and Memories from your iPhone's photo library.

1. Launch the Apple Watch app on your iPhone.
2. Access My Watch > Photos, and enable Sync Memories and Sync Featured Photos.

PAUSING PHOTO SYNCING

If you want to stop your iPhone from syncing Memories, featured photos, or photos from a chosen album, follow these steps:

1. Open the Apple Watch app on your iPhone.
2. Go to My Watch > Photos, and turn off Photo Syncing.

MANAGING PHOTO STORAGE

The quantity of photos stored on your Apple Watch depends on available space. To allocate space for other content, you can limit the number of photos stored.

1. Open the Apple Watch app on your iPhone.
2. Visit My Watch > Photos > Photos Limit.

TO VIEW THE NUMBER OF PHOTOS ON YOUR APPLE WATCH

- On your Apple Watch: Go to General > About in the Settings app .
- On your iPhone: Access General > About in the Apple Watch app.

TAKING SCREENSHOTS ON APPLE WATCH

1. On your Apple Watch, navigate to Settings > General > Screenshots, and tap Enable Screenshots.
2. To capture a screenshot, simultaneously press the Digital Crown and the side button. Screenshots are saved in your iPhone's Photos app for later viewing.

VIEWING PHOTOS AND MEMORIES ON APPLE WATCH

Exploring Photos in the Photos App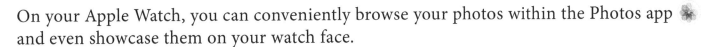

On your Apple Watch, you can conveniently browse your photos within the Photos app 🌸 and even showcase them on your watch face.

Tap to view a photo.

BROWSING PHOTOS

Open the Photos app 🌸 on your Apple Watch and use the following steps to navigate through your photos.

1. Tap on a memory, Featured Photos, or an album that you've synced to your Apple Watch.
2. Tap on a specific photo to open and view it.
3. Swipe left or right to navigate between different photos.
   - Use the Digital Crown to zoom in or out on a photo, and drag to move around within a photo.
   - Zoom out completely to see the entire album of photos.

Swipe left or right to see the next photo.

Turn to zoom.

Drag to pan.

Double-tap to fill screen or see all.

VIEWING MEMORIES ON WATCH FACES

Aside from checking out Memories in the Photos app 🌸 , you can also enjoy them on the Siri and Photos watch faces.

- To see a recent memory on the Siri watch face, select the Siri watch face and tap on a memory.
- To view photos from Memories on the Photos watch face, access the Apple Watch app on your iPhone, go to Face Gallery, choose the Photos watch face, and select Dynamic.

  - The Dynamic watch face will showcase images from your recent Memories, updating with new ones.

VIEWING LIVE PHOTOS

Find the Live Photo ◎ in the bottom-left corner of a picture. To experience a Live Photo, touch and hold the photo.

SHARING PHOTOS

While viewing a photo in the Photos app on your Apple Watch, tap on ⬆ , then pick a sharing option that suits you.

CREATING A PHOTO WATCH FACE

While viewing a photo within the Photos app 🌸 on your Apple Watch, tap on ⬆ , scroll down, and then tap Create Face. If you prefer, you can also generate a Kaleidoscope watch face inspired by the photo, or include a new Photos watch face using the Apple Watch app on your iPhone. To learn more, explore the Customize the Watch Face section.

Note: For added convenience, you can efficiently design a watch face on your iPhone. Launch the Photos app on your iPhone, select a photo, tap on , swipe up, click on Create Watch Face, and decide whether to create a Portraits, Photos, or Kaleidoscope watch face.

PODCASTS

Listening to Podcasts on Apple Watch:

The Podcasts app on Apple Watch shows podcast artwork. Tap the artwork to play the episode.

ADDING PODCASTS TO APPLE WATCH

By adding podcasts to your Apple Watch, you can enjoy them even when your iPhone is not around. You can achieve this via the Apple Watch app on your iPhone or directly on your Apple Watch.

USING YOUR IPHONE

When you follow podcasts and create stations in the Podcasts app on your iPhone, recent episodes from those shows can be downloaded to your Apple Watch when it's connected to a power source. Refer to the iPhone User Guide for details on following podcasts and creating stations.

1. Launch the Apple Watch app on your iPhone.
2. Go to My Watch, tap Podcasts, and then take any of the following actions:
- To add episodes from stations: Under Add Episodes From, tap Up Next, Saved, or a specific station, and then choose the number of episodes to download to your Apple Watch.
- To add episodes from podcasts you follow: Under Shows, select Add Shows, tap ⊕ next to the desired shows, and tap Done.

Your Apple Watch will automatically add three episodes of each show when connected to power. You can modify this by tapping on a show and selecting your preferred number of episodes.

FOLLOWING AND UNFOLLOWING PODCASTS WITH APPLE WATCH

1. Open the Podcasts app 🎙 on your Apple Watch.
2. Try the following:
   - Tap Listen Now, tap You Might Like, choose a show, and tap Follow.
   - Tap Search, enter the podcast name, select the show, and tap Follow.
3. Tap on ●●●, then set the number of episodes to download when your Apple Watch connects to power.

To unfollow a show, tap Library, choose the show, tap ↓, and then select Unfollow Show.

ACCESSING DOWNLOADED PODCASTS

1. Open the Podcasts app 🎙 on your Apple Watch.
2. Tap Library, and then tap Downloaded.

LISTENING TO PODCASTS

You can enjoy podcasts stored on your Apple Watch or stream them from your iPhone.

1. Connect Bluetooth headphones or speakers to your Apple Watch.
2. Proceed with the following options:
   - Scroll through the artwork and tap a podcast to play it.
   - Tap Library, tap Downloaded, and select a podcast to play it.
   - Tap On iPhone, choose a category, locate an episode, and tap to play it.

STREAMING PODCASTS

If your Apple Watch is near your iPhone or connected to Wi-Fi or cellular (for compatible models), you can stream podcasts.

Open the Podcasts app 🎙 on your Apple Watch and do the following:
- Stream from your library: Tap Library, choose a show, tap See All, and then tap an episode.
- Explore suggested podcasts: Tap Listen Now, scroll down, tap a category, and select an episode.
- Search for a podcast: Tap Search, enter the podcast name, tap Search, select a result, and tap an episode.

USING SIRI TO PLAY PODCASTS

Activate Siri and say something like "Hey Siri, play the podcast [Podcast Name]." Siri will play the latest episode of the requested podcast.

MANAGING PLAYBACK

You can control playback directly on your Apple Watch

- Adjust volume using the Digital Crown.
- Play, pause, skip forward 30 seconds, skip back 15 seconds.
- Change playback speed (1x, 1 1/2x, 2x, and 1/2x).
- Choose an episode from the currently playing podcast.

View more episodes.

Change playback speed.

Choose playback option

▶	Play the current podcast.
⏸	Pause playback.
⟳30	Skip ahead 30 seconds.
⟲15	Skip back 15 seconds.
1x	Playback speed. Options include 1x, 1 1/2x, 2x, and 1/2x.
☰	Choose an episode of the currently playing podcast.

CUSTOMIZING PODCAST SETTINGS

You can customize Podcasts settings on your Apple Watch:

1. Open the Settings app ⚙ on your Apple Watch.
2. Tap Podcasts and adjust settings like Up Next, Saved, Continuous Playback, Skip buttons interval, and more.

REMINDERS

Your Apple Watch keeps you updated on reminders you set up in the Reminders app on your Apple Watch, iPhone, and other Apple devices where you're signed in with your Apple ID. If you want to know how to set up the Reminders app on your iPhone, consult the iPhone User Guide.

VIEWING AND MANAGING REMINDERS

1. Open the Reminders app ⊕ on your Apple Watch.
2. Tap a list to access it.
3. To mark a reminder as completed, tap ◯ on the left side of an item, or tap the reminder and then tap Mark as Completed.
4. Use the < in the top-left corner to return to the list view.
5. To see completed reminders, tap a list, choose View Options, and tap Show Completed.
   • To view all completed reminders, tap the All list, select View Options, and tap Show Completed.
   • To adjust the order of your lists, open the Reminders app on your iPhone, tap Edit, and then drag the list to a new location.

SHARING AND COLLABORATING ON LISTS

You can collaborate with others who use iCloud by sharing a list. Shared lists indicate who a reminder is assigned to. On your Apple Watch, you can join a shared list, but you can't create a shared list from the watch. For more details on shared reminder lists, refer to the iPhone User Guide.

Turn to see more lists.

Tap to view the items.

RESPONDING TO REMINDER NOTIFICATIONS

- If you receive a reminder notification: Tap the notification, swipe (or turn the Digital crown to scroll) the reminder, then tap Mark as Completed or choose a reminder time.
- If you notice the notification later: Locate it in your list of notifications, and then respond accordingly.

CREATING REMINDERS

- Use Siri: Speak a command like "Remind me to pick up my dry cleaning at 5 PM." You can also utilize Siri to create a list directly on your Apple Watch.
- Use the Reminders app: Scroll to the bottom of any list, and tap Add Reminder.

DELETING AND EDITING REMINDERS

1. Open the Reminders app ⚙ on your Apple Watch.
2. Access a list, then either swipe left on the reminder and tap 🗑, or tap the reminder, scroll down, and tap Delete.

EDITING A REMINDER

You can edit reminders on your self-set Apple Watch

1. Open the Reminders app ⚙ on your Apple Watch.
2. Access a list, tap a Reminder, tap Edit, and then perform any of the following actions:

- Change the reminder's name using the keyboard options available (QWERTY, QuickPath, Scribble, or emoji). Note: QuickPath is only available on Apple Watch Series 7 and Apple Watch Series 8.
- Add a note.
- Set a date and time, with options to repeat the reminder.
- Include a tag or create a new one.
- Add a location-based reminder, for example, when arriving home or connecting to a Bluetooth-enabled car.
- Flag the reminder.
- Select a priority level.
- Assign the reminder to a different list.

REMOTE

Using Apple Watch to Control Music and Apple TV

CONTROLLING MUSIC ON A MAC OR PC

Utilize the Remote app on your Apple Watch to manage music playback on a computer within the same Wi-Fi network.

ADDING A MUSIC LIBRARY

1. Open the Remote app ▶ on your Apple Watch.
2. Tap Add Device.
   - If you're using the Music app on macOS 10.15 or later: Launch Apple Music and select your device from the list displayed alongside your library.
   - If you're using iTunes on your Mac or PC: Click the Remote button located near the top left of the iTunes window.
3. Enter the displayed 4-digit code on your Apple Watch.

PLAYBACK CONTROL FROM APPLE WATCH

You can control playback in the following ways:
- Utilize playback controls available in the Remote app ▶.
- Adjust volume using the Digital Crown.
- Tap ⦿, then choose an audio output.

SELECTING A MEDIA LIBRARY

- If you've added multiple libraries: Choose the desired one when opening the Remote app ▶ on your Apple Watch.
- If music is already playing: Tap < at the top left of the playback controls and then select the library.

REMOVING A MEDIA LIBRARY

1. Open the Remote app ▶ on your Apple Watch.
2. Long-press a device.
3. Once the device icon starts jiggling, tap X to remove it, then tap Remove.

APPLE TV CONTROL WITH APPLE WATCH

Your Apple Watch can function as a remote for an Apple TV when both are connected to the same Wi-Fi network.

PAIRING APPLE WATCH WITH APPLE TV

If your iPhone has never joined the Apple TV's Wi-Fi network, follow these steps:
1. Open the Remote app  on your Apple Watch.
2. Tap your Apple TV. If it's not listed, tap Add Device.
3. On the Apple TV, navigate to Settings > Remotes and Devices > Remote App and Devices, and choose Apple Watch.
4. Enter the passcode displayed on your Apple Watch.
   - Once the pairing icon appears next to your Apple Watch, it's ready to control the Apple TV.

USING APPLE WATCH TO CONTROL APPLE TV

Ensure the Apple TV is awake and follow these steps:
1. Open the Remote app on your Apple Watch.
2. Select your Apple TV and swipe in various directions to navigate the menu.
3. Tap to select the highlighted item.
4. Use the Play/Pause button to pause or resume playback.
5. Press the Menu button to return or hold it to access the main menu.

To initiate the screen saver, move to the top-left corner of the Apple TV's Home Screen and tap the Menu button.

Control another device.

10:09

SELECT

Swipe to move through Apple TV menu options; tap to select.

Tap to go back or touch and hold to return to main menu.

UNPAIRING AND REMOVING APPLE TV

1. On the Apple TV, navigate to Settings > Remotes and Devices > Remote App and Devices.
2. Choose your Apple Watch under Remote App, then select Unpair Device.
3. Open the Remote app on your Apple Watch and tap Remove when the "lost connection" message appears.

SLEEP

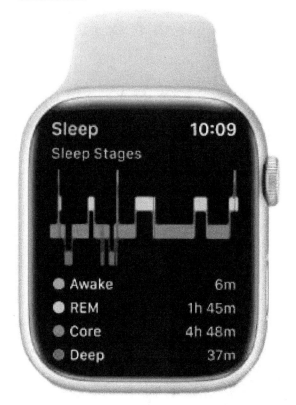

SLEEP TRACKING WITH APPLE WATCH

The Sleep app on Apple Watch empowers you to establish bedtime routines that aid in achieving your sleep targets. Don your watch before sleep, and it will estimate the duration spent in various sleep stages: REM, Core, and Deep. It can also provide insights into when you might have awakened. Upon waking up, access the Sleep app to view your sleep duration and trends across the last 14 days.

BATTERY CHARGE ALERT

When your Apple Watch charge drops below 30 percent before bedtime, a reminder will prompt you to recharge it. In the morning, simply check the greeting to assess the remaining battery charge.

SLEEP SCHEDULING

Apple Watch tracks your sleep as per the customized sleep schedule you establish. You can also manually activate Sleep Focus to minimize disturbances before and after sleep. To garner sleep data, Apple Watch must track your sleep for a **minimum of four hours** each night.

MULTIPLE SCHEDULES OPTION

You can create various schedules, tailored for different days. Each schedule allows for the following settings:

- Set a sleep goal (desired sleep hours)
- Determine bedtime and wake-up time
- Choose an alarm sound for waking up
- Specify when to activate Sleep Focus (limiting pre-sleep distractions)
- Enable sleep tracking, which utilizes your movement to detect sleep during sleep hours with active Sleep Focus

DISABLING SLEEP FOCUS

Press and hold the Digital Crown to unlock your device and swipe up to open Control Center. Tap 🛏 to disable Sleep Focus.

ENABLING SLEEP ON APPLE WATCH

1. Launch the Sleep app 🛏 on your Apple Watch.
2. Follow the on-screen instructions.

Alternatively, you can access the Health app ♥ on your iPhone, tap Browse, select Sleep, and then tap Get Started under Set Up Sleep.

ADJUSTING OR DISABLING WAKE-UP ALARM

1. Open the Sleep app 🛏 on your Apple Watch.
2. Tap your existing wake-up time.
3. To modify the wake-up time, turn the Digital Crown to set a new time and tap   .

If you wish to disable the wake-up alarm, turn off Alarm. Alternatively, you can use the Health app on your iPhone, tap Browse, choose Sleep, and tap Edit under Your Schedule to make adjustments.

These changes only change the forthcoming wake-up alarm; your regular schedule resumes afterward.

ALTERNATE DISABLING METHOD

You can also turn off the next wake-up alarm within the Alarms app 🕐 . Locate the alarm under Sleep | Wake up, tap it, and then select Skip for Tonight.

ADJUSTING OR ADDING A SLEEP SCHEDULE:

CHANGE OR ADD A SLEEP SCHEDULE

1. Launch the Sleep app 🛏 on your Apple Watch.
2. Tap Full Schedule, and proceed with one of the following actions:
   - To modify an existing sleep schedule, tap the current schedule.
   - To introduce a new sleep schedule, tap Add Schedule.
   - For altering sleep goal, tap Sleep Goal, and specify your desired sleep duration.
   - To adjust Wind Down time, tap Wind Down, and define how long Sleep Focus should activate before bedtime. Sleep Focus darkens the watch display and activates Do Not Disturb to minimize distractions prior to sleep.
3. There are extra customizations including:
   - Set Days for the Schedule: Access your schedule, tap Active On, select days, and tap <.
   - Adjust Wake Time and Bedtime: Within your schedule, tap Wake Up or Bedtime, use the Digital Crown to set new times, and tap ✅ .
   - Set Alarm Options: In your schedule, control Alarm by toggling it on or off and selecting Sound & Haptics to choose an alarm sound.
   - Remove or Cancel a Schedule: To eliminate an existing schedule, tap your schedule and tap Delete Schedule at the bottom. To cancel creating a new one, tap Cancel at the top.

MODIFYING SLEEP SETTINGS

1. Access the Settings app ⚙ on your Apple Watch.
2. Tap Sleep, and proceed to customize the following settings:
   - Turn On at Wind Down: If you'd rather manage Sleep Focus manually in Control Center, disable this option.
   - Sleep Screen: Simplify the Apple Watch display and iPhone Lock Screen during Sleep Focus to minimize distractions.
   - Show Time: Display the date and time on your Apple Watch and iPhone during Sleep Focus.
1. Toggle Sleep Tracking and Charging Reminders on or off.
   - When Sleep Tracking is enabled, Apple Watch records sleep data in the Health app on your iPhone.
   - Activating Charging Reminders results in reminders to charge your watch before Wind Down time and notifications when your watch is fully charged.

REVIEWING SLEEP HISTORY

1. Launch the Sleep app 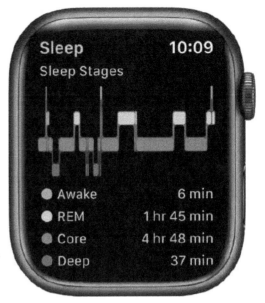 on your Apple Watch.
2. Scroll down to view the previous night's sleep duration, time spent in sleep stages, and a 14-day sleep average.

EVALUATING RESPIRATORY RATE:

Use your Apple Watch to monitor your breathing rate during sleep, which can provide valuable health insights.

1. Open the Health app on your iPhone, tap Browse, then tap Respiratory.
2. Select Respiratory Rate and tap Show More Respiratory Rate Data to view your sleep-related breathing patterns.

MONITORING WRIST TEMPERATURE WITH APPLE WATCH SERIES 8

Wear your Apple Watch Series 8 during sleep to track changes in wrist temperature, aiding well-being assessment.

1. Ensure Track Sleep with Apple Watch is enabled.
2. To establish a baseline, activate Sleep Focus and wear your watch while sleeping.
   • Wrist temperature data becomes available after about five nights.

REVIEWING WRIST TEMPERATURE

1. Open the Health app  on your iPhone, tap Browse.
2. Navigate to Body Measurements and tap Wrist Temperature.
3. Tap a chart point for detailed sample information.

DEACTIVATING WRIST TEMPERATURE TRACKING

1. Open the Apple Watch app on your iPhone.
2. Tap My Watch, proceed to Privacy, and toggle off Wrist Temperature.

STOCKS

MONITORING STOCKS WITH THE STOCKS APP

Utilize the Stocks app on your Apple Watch to access information about stocks you follow on your iPhone. For comprehensive guidance on using the Stocks app on your iPhone, refer to the iPhone User Guide.

USING SIRI FOR STOCK INFORMATION

You can also obtain stock information via Siri. For instance, ask Siri questions like: "What was today's closing price for Apple stock?"

ADDING AND REMOVING STOCKS

Manage your tracked stocks directly from your Apple Watch. Follow these steps within the Stocks app on your watch:

- To add a stock: Scroll to the bottom, tap Add Stock. Input the stock name using text entry, Scribble (available on Apple Watch Series 7 and 8), or dictation. Confirm the selection.
- To remove a stock: Swipe left on the stock you wish to remove, then tap X. For rearranging stock order, tap and hold a stock, and drag it to the desired position.
- Rearranging stocks on one device automatically applies changes to the other.

VIEWING STOCK DATA

1. Launch the Stocks app  on your Apple Watch.
2. Tap a stock to access its data.
3. To return to the stock list, tap <, or use the Digital Crown to navigate to the next stock in the list.

SELECTING STOCKS FOR SIRI WATCH FACE

1. Open the Settings app ⚙ on your Apple Watch.
2. Navigate to Stocks > Selected Stock, and make a selection.

CUSTOMIZING DATA METRICS

Tailor the data metrics displayed in the Stocks app, complications, and the Siri watch face by following these steps:

- To modify the data metric in the Stocks app: Open the Stocks app 〰 on your Apple Watch, tap Viewing, and choose Points, Market Cap, or Percentage.
- For changing the data metric on Stocks complications and the Siri watch face: In the Settings app ⚙ on your Apple Watch, tap Stocks > Data Metric, and select a metric. You can also adjust this setting via the Apple Watch app on your iPhone.

SWITCHING TO STOCKS ON IPHONE

1. Access the Stocks app 〰 on your Apple Watch.
2. On your iPhone, access the App Switcher by swiping up from the bottom edge and pausing (Face ID devices) or double-clicking the Home button (Home button devices).
3. Tap the displayed button at the bottom of the screen to open the Stocks app on your iPhone.

STOPWATCH

PRECISELY TIME EVENTS WITH EASE

Effortlessly time events with Apple Watch's accuracy. It can track entire events up to 11 hours and 55 minutes, recording lap or split times. Results can be presented as a list, a graph, or displayed live on your watch face. The Chronograph and Chronograph Pro watch faces include the built-in stopwatch feature.

OPENING AND SELECTING A STOPWATCH

1. Open the Stopwatch app  on your Apple Watch, or tap the stopwatch directly on your watch face (if it's added or you're using the Chronograph or Chronograph Pro watch face).
2. Choose from Analog, Digital, Graph, or Hybrid formats on the Stopwatch screen.
3. To switch to a different format while viewing the stopwatch, tap < and select your preferred format.

STARTING, STOPPING, AND RESETTING THE STOPWATCH

Open the Stopwatch app  on your Apple Watch, pick a format, and perform these actions:
- To start timing: Tap the Start button (usually green on the analog stopwatch).
- To record a lap time: Tap the Lap button (typically white on the analog stopwatch).
- To finalize the time: Tap the Stop button (usually red on the analog stopwatch).
- To reset the stopwatch: If the stopwatch is stopped, tap the Reset button (typically white on the analog stopwatch).

Start or stop the stopwatch.

Record lap times.

CONTINUOUS TIMING

Even if you switch back to the watch face or access other apps, the stopwatch will continue running in the background.

REVIEWING AND ANALYZING RESULTS

After timing an event, you can review the results on the same display you used for timing. Alternatively, you can switch displays to examine your lap times. Fastest and slowest laps are indicated with green and red markers. If the display shows a list of lap times, use the Digital Crown to scroll through them.

TIMERS

Apple Watch's Timers app helps you manage time effectively. You can establish multiple timers, each capable of tracking time for up to 24 hours.

USING SIRI FOR TIMERS

Simply ask Siri to set a timer. For instance, say "Set a timer for 20 minutes."

QUICK TIMER SETUP

1. Open the Timers app ⏱ on your Apple Watch.
2. To swiftly start a timer, tap a predefined duration (like 1, 3, or 5 minutes) or select a timer from your recent ones below Recents.
   - For a custom timer, swipe down and tap Custom.
   - When one timer ends, you can quickly restart a timer with the same duration by tapping ⏱.

PAUSING AND ENDING TIMERS

1. When a timer is running, access the Timers app on your Apple Watch.
2. Tap ❙❙ to pause, tap ▶ to resume, or tap ✕ to conclude the timer.

CREATING A PERSONALIZED TIMER

1. Open the Timers app 🕑 on your Apple Watch.
2. Scroll up and tap Custom.
3. Adjust hours, minutes, or seconds using the Digital Crown.
4. Tap Start to initiate the custom timer.

Tap hours, minutes, or seconds, then turn the Digital Crown.

MANAGING MULTIPLE TIMERS

1. Access the Timers app 🕑 on your Apple Watch.
2. Create and initiate a timer.
   • Use Siri to label timers, such as "Pizza." Just say, "Set a 12-minute pizza timer."
3. Return to the Timers screen by tapping <, then set up additional timers.
   • All ongoing timers are displayed on the Timers screen. Pause with a tap and resume with .
   • To delete a running or paused timer, swipe left and tap X.

FAVORITE TIMERS

1. Open the Timers app 🕑 on your Apple Watch.
2. Swipe left on a recent timer, then tap ⭐.
   • The timer becomes a favorite and is listed under the Favorites section.

VOICE MEMOS

Utilize the Voice Memos app  on your Apple Watch to conveniently record personal notes and thoughts.

RECORDING A VOICE MEMO

1. Open the Voice Memos app on your Apple Watch.
2. Tap the record button to commence recording.
3. Tap the stop button to conclude the recording.

LISTENING TO A VOICE MEMO

1. Access the Voice Memos app on your Apple Watch.
2. Tap on a recording displayed on the Voice Memos screen.
3. To initiate playback, tap the play button   .

EDITING AND DELETING RECORDINGS

1. Open the Voice Memos app on your Apple Watch.
2. Select a recording from the Voice Memos screen.
3. To modify the recording's name, tap , then choose Edit Name.
   - To delete the recording, tap ●●●, then select Delete.

SYNCING YOUR VOICE MEMOS

Voice memos you record on your Apple Watch are automatically synchronized with your other devices, including Mac, iPad, and iOS devices where you're signed in using the same Apple ID.

WALKIE TALKIE

Experience the joy of communicating with another compatible Apple Watch user through the Walkie-Talkie feature. This simple and enjoyable method operates like a traditional walkie-talkie.

Press a button to talk, release to listen, and wait for the response. Both participants need connectivity, either via Bluetooth connection to an iPhone, Wi-Fi, or cellular. It's important to note that Walkie-Talkie might not be available in all regions.

INVITING A FRIEND

1. Launch the Walkie-Talkie app 🔘 on your Apple Watch for the first time.
2. Browse the list of contacts and tap a name to send an invitation.

After your friend accepts the invitation, you can initiate Walkie-Talkie conversations whenever both of you are available. To add more contacts, tap "Add Friends" on the Walkie-Talkie screen and select a contact.

ENGAGING IN A WALKIE-TALKIE CHAT

1. Open the Walkie-Talkie app on your Apple Watch.
2. Tap your friend's name.
3. Hold down the Talk button and speak.

If your friend is available, their Apple Watch will open the Walkie-Talkie app, allowing them to hear your message. Adjust your speaking volume using the Digital Crown.

TALKING WITH A SINGLE TAP

If pressing and holding the Talk button is challenging, you can enable single-tap talking.

1. Access the Settings app on your Apple Watch.
2. Tap Accessibility and turn on "Tap to Talk" below Walkie-Talkie.
Once enabled, tap once to talk and tap again to finish speaking. This setting can also be adjusted in the Apple Watch app on your iPhone under Accessibility.

MANAGING CONTACTS

To remove contacts

In the Walkie-Talkie app , swipe left on a contact and tap X.

SETTING YOURSELF AS UNAVAILABLE

1. Swipe up on the screen to open Control Center.
2. Scroll down and tap .

Alternatively, open the Walkie-Talkie app and scroll to the top of the screen, then turn off Walkie-Talkie. Activating theater mode also makes you unavailable for Walkie-Talkie.

WALLET & APPLE PAY

UNDERSTANDING WALLET ON APPLE WATCH

The Wallet app is designed to provide convenient access to your cards and passes in one location. Wallet can hold a variety of items, including:

- Apple Pay cards like Apple Card and Apple Cash (Refer to "Set up Apple Pay" for more details)
- Transit cards (Learn about using transit cards)
- Digital keys (See how to use digital keys)
- Driver's license or state ID (Discover using your driver's license or state ID)
- Employee badges (Accessing your workplace credentials)
- Student ID cards (Using contactless passes or student ID cards)
- Rewards cards, boarding passes, and event tickets (Using Wallet for passes)
- Vaccination records (Understanding COVID-19 vaccination cards)

APPLE PAY ON APPLE WATCH

Apple Pay ensures a simple, secure, and private payment method on your Apple Watch. By storing your cards in the Wallet app on your iPhone and adding them to your Apple Watch, you can leverage Apple Pay in various ways:

- Contactless payments and apps: Utilize credit, debit, and prepaid cards added to the Wallet app to make purchases at stores supporting contactless payments and within apps compatible with Apple Pay.

Upon setting up Apple Pay in the Apple Watch app on your iPhone, you're equipped for in-store purchases, even without your iPhone present. (Apple Pay availability varies by region.)

- Person-to-person payments: In watchOS 4 and later versions, you can seamlessly send and request money securely via Messages or Siri.
- Transit cards: Add transit cards, which appear at the top of your collection in the Wallet app , above your passes.

For up-to-date information regarding Apple Pay availability and participating card issuers, consult the Apple Support article titled "Apple Pay Participating Banks."

IMPORTANT CONSIDERATIONS

Note: Unpairing your Apple Watch or deactivating your passcode will result in the inability to use Apple Pay, and any cards stored in Wallet will be removed. If wrist detection is turned off, you'll need to enter your passcode each time you use Apple Pay.

SETTING UP APPLE PAY ON YOUR APPLE WATCH

ADDING A CARD VIA YOUR IPHONE

1. Launch the Apple Watch app on your iPhone.
2. Select "My Watch" and then tap on "Wallet & Apple Pay."
3. If you already possess cards on your other Apple devices or recently removed cards, tap "Add" next to the card you wish to include. Input the card's CVV.
4. For any other card, choose "Add Card" and proceed by following the onscreen prompts.

Please note that your card provider might require additional verification steps to confirm your identity.

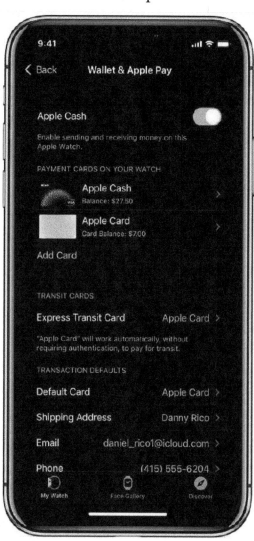

ADDING A CARD DIRECTLY ON APPLE WATCH

You have the convenience of adding Apple Account, credit, debit, and transit cards directly on your Apple Watch.

1. Open the Wallet app on your Apple Watch.
2. Scroll down to the bottom of the screen and tap "Add Card."
3. Select between Apple Account, Debit or Credit Card, or Transit Card, and then proceed by following the instructions displayed on the screen.

111

MANAGING APPLE PAY ON YOUR APPLE WATCH

SELECTING YOUR DEFAULT CARD

1. Access the Apple Watch app on your iPhone.
2. Tap "My Watch," followed by "Wallet & Apple Pay."
3. Tap "Default Card," and then choose the desired card.

REARRANGING PAYMENT CARDS

Open the Wallet app on your Apple Watch, press and hold a card, and drag it to a new position. For managed Apple Watches, this applies to both payment cards and passes.

REMOVING A CARD FROM APPLE PAY

1. Launch the Wallet app on your Apple Watch.
2. Select a card by tapping it.
3. Scroll down and tap "Remove."

You can also perform this action via the Apple Watch app on your iPhone by tapping "My Watch," "Wallet & Apple Pay," selecting the card, and then tapping "Remove Card."

FINDING THE DEVICE ACCOUNT NUMBER

When you make a payment using your Apple Watch, the Device Account Number is sent along with the payment. To find the last four digits of this number:

1. Open the Wallet app on your Apple Watch.
2. Tap a card to select it, then tap "Card Information."
Note: For Apple Card, you must enter your Apple Watch passcode before accessing card details. This can also be done via the Apple Watch app on your iPhone.

MODIFYING DEFAULT TRANSACTION DETAILS

You can customize your in-app transaction preferences, such as default card, shipping address, email, and phone number:

1. Launch the Apple Watch app on your iPhone.
2. Tap "My Watch," then "Wallet & Apple Pay."
3. Scroll down and tap "Transaction Defaults." Edit any desired item.

IN CASE OF LOST OR STOLEN APPLE WATCH

If your Apple Watch is lost or stolen, consider the following steps:

- Activate lost mode to halt the ability to pay from your Apple Watch.
- Sign in to appleid.apple.com with your Apple ID to remove the ability to pay using cards in Wallet. Under Devices, choose your device and click "Remove All" under Apple Pay.
- Contact your card issuers for further assistance.

MAKING PAYMENTS WITH APPLE WATCH

Paying in-store:
1. Double-click the side button.
2. Scroll and choose a card.
3. Hold your Apple Watch close to the contactless card reader, display facing it.

A gentle tap and beep indicate the payment was sent. A confirmation notification arrives in Notification Center.

MAKING IN-APP PURCHASES

1. While in an app on your Apple Watch, opt for the Apple Pay choice during checkout.
2. Review details and double-click the side button to pay.

SENDING, RECEIVING, AND REQUESTING MONEY WITH APPLE WATCH

Sending Money with Apple Cash

Apart from using Apple Cash for in-store purchases, you can effortlessly send money to friends and family. This can be done through messages or even Siri. Receiving and requesting money is just as straightforward.

Note: Apple Cash is limited to certain regions and supports iPhone SE and iPhone 6 models and later. For comprehensive information on Apple Pay and Apple Cash, refer to the iPhone User Guide.

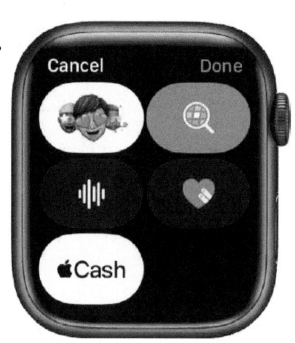

SENDING A PAYMENT FROM APPLE WATCH

Use Siri: Voice a command like "Send $25 to Claire." If you have multiple contacts named Claire, you'll be prompted to pick the intended one.

1. Launch the Messages app ⬭ on your Apple Watch.
2. Initiate a new conversation or select an existing one, then tap ⬭, followed by ⬭.
3. Use the Digital Crown or plus/minus buttons to select a whole dollar amount. For fractional amounts (e.g., $10.95), tap the dollar value, then tap the amount after the decimal and adjust using the Digital Crown.
4. Confirm and send the payment by double-clicking the side button. Upon successful payment, a confirmation message appears.

The payment is initially debited from your Apple Cash balance. If this balance is insufficient, the remaining sum is drawn from your linked debit card.

CANCELING A PAYMENT

You can cancel a payment if the recipient hasn't accepted it yet.
1. Access the Wallet app ⬭ on your Apple Watch.
2. Choose a card by tapping it, then scroll through your transaction list.
3. Tap the pending transaction, and then tap "Cancel Payment."

This action can also be performed through the Apple Watch app on your iPhone: "My Watch" > "Wallet & Apple Pay" > Apple Cash card > "Transactions" > unpaid transaction > "Cancel Payment."

REQUESTING PAYMENT

You can initiate payment requests using Siri or messages.
- Via Siri: "Ask James to send me $30."
- Using Messages: Launch the Messages app ⬭ on your Apple Watch, start a new conversation or select an existing one, then tap ⬭, followed by ⬭Cash. Swipe left on the Send button, input the amount, and tap Request.

Upon your first usage of Apple Cash, you need to agree to the terms and conditions on your iPhone before accepting payments. Subsequent payments are automatically accepted, unless you prefer manual acceptance. To alter this setting, open Wallet on your iPhone, tap the Apple Cash card, tap •••, and then tap "Manually Accept Payments."

RESPONDING TO A PAYMENT REQUEST

1. Tap the Send button displayed in the payment request within Messages.
2. Change the amount by turning the Digital Crown or tapping on-screen buttons, if desired.
3. Send the payment by tapping Send and double-clicking the side button.

VIEWING TRANSACTION DETAILS

- In Messages: Open the Messages app ⭕ on your Apple Watch and tap on an Apple Pay essage to access a transaction summary.
- In Wallet: Launch the Wallet app 🔘 on your Apple Watch, tap a card, and scroll through the list of transactions. Tap a transaction for more information.

To review your complete Apple Cash transaction history on your iPhone, access the Apple Watch app, navigate to "My Watch," tap "Wallet & Apple Pay," select your Apple Cash card, tap "Transactions," and swipe to the bottom to request a transaction statement via email.

MANAGING APPLE CASH WITH APPLE WATCH (U.S. ONLY)

RECEIVING AND USING APPLE CASH

When you receive money through Apple Cash, the funds are added to your Apple Cash card within the Wallet. You can utilize Apple Cash immediately for transactions where you would typically use Apple Pay—whether in stores, apps, or online. Additionally, it's possible to transfer your Apple Cash balance to your bank account. If you're responsible for a family sharing group, you can set up Apple Cash Family for family members.

MANAGING APPLE CASH PAYMENT FEATURES

Navigate to the Apple Watch app on your iPhone, tap "My Watch," then select "Wallet & Apple Pay." Here, you can perform the following actions:
- Tap the Apple Cash card to initiate setup. If Apple Cash is already configured on another device, it will be ready for use on your Apple Watch.
- Enable or disable the Apple Cash card, as well as the ability to send and receive money, on this particular device.
- View your suggested PIN, which can also be accessed on your Apple Watch through the Wallet app 🔘 . Scroll down on your Apple Cash card and tap "Card Information." A PIN isn't necessary for Apple Cash, as payments are authenticated by Face ID, Touch ID, or a secure passcode. However, some terminals may still require a four-digit code to finalize a transaction.
- Check your Apple Cash balance by opening the Wallet app 🔘 on your Apple Watch

and selecting your Apple Cash card. Alternatively, double-click the side button and scroll to the Apple Cash card.
- Manage Apple Cash Family for family members under 18.

Please note that person-to-person payments with Apple Pay and Apple Cash are subject to regional availability.
Apple Cash and the sending and receiving of payments through Apple Pay are services offered by Green Dot Bank, an FDIC member.

ADDING AND USING PASSES IN WALLET ON APPLE WATCH

Leverage the Wallet app  on your Apple Watch to store and access your boarding passes, event tickets, coupons, student ID cards, and more conveniently. Passes that you have on your Wallet app on the iPhone are automatically synchronized to your Apple Watch. This allows you to utilize passes on your watch for actions such as flight check-ins, coupon redemptions, and access to certain areas.

CUSTOMIZING PASS OPTIONS

1. Open the Apple Watch app on your iPhone.
2. Tap "My Watch," then select "Wallet & Apple Pay."

ADDING A PASS

To include a pass, use any of the following methods:
- Follow the instructions received via email from the issuer.
- Utilize the pass issuer's dedicated app, if available.
- Tap "Add" in the notification.
- If you receive a pass via Messages, tap to add it.

USING A PASS

You can seamlessly employ various passes on your Apple Watch.
- When a pass notification appears on your Apple Watch, tap it to display the pass. If necessary, scroll to access the barcode.
- For barcode passes, double-click the side button, scroll to your pass, and present the barcode to the scanner. Alternatively, open the Wallet app on your Apple Watch, select the pass, and scan it.

ACCESSING PASS INFORMATION

To retrieve additional details about a pass—like flight departure and arrival times—perform these steps:

1. Open the Wallet app 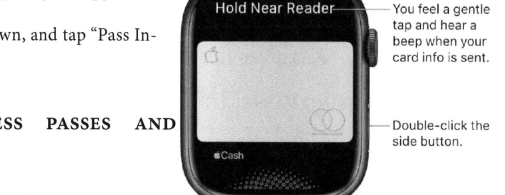 on your Apple Watch.
2. Select a pass, scroll down, and tap "Pass Information."

USING CONTACTLESS PASSES AND STUDENT ID CARDS

With a contactless pass or student ID card, you can present your Apple Watch to a contactless reader for verification.

- If a contactless pass notification appears, tap it. If not, double-click the side button and hold your Apple Watch close to the reader.
- For student ID cards on supported campuses, simply place your Apple Watch near the reader, with the display facing it, until your watch vibrates—there's no need to double-click the side button.

REORDERING AND REMOVING PASSES

On your Apple Watch, use the Wallet app to rearrange transit, access, payment cards, and passes. Dragging a payment card to the top slot designates it as the default payment card.

On a managed Apple Watch, you can reorder all types of passes. To remove a pass, double-click the side button, select the pass, scroll down, and tap "Delete." Alternatively, open the Wallet app on your iPhone, tap the pass, tap , and choose "Remove Pass." Removing a pass on one device will also remove it from the other.

VIEWING EXPIRED PASSES

Expired passes are hidden to keep things organized on your Apple Watch. To see these passes:

1. Open the Wallet app on your Apple Watch.
2. Scroll to the bottom and tap "View [number] Expired Passes."
3. Select a pass to view its details, and unhide, share, or delete it if needed.

To continuously display expired passes, open the Settings app on your Apple Watch, tap "Wallet & Apple Pay," and turn off "Hide Expired Passes."

USING REWARDS CARDS ON APPLE WATCH:

ADDING REWARDS CARDS

If you possess a rewards card from a merchant that supports this feature, you can conveniently include it in your Wallet and effortlessly present it to a contactless reader •cash :transactions using your Apple Watch.

ADDING A REWARDS CARD TO APPLE WATCH

You can add a rewards card to Wallet through different methods:
- Email or Website Link: If you come across an "Add to Apple Wallet" link in an email or on a website, tap the link to add the rewards card.
- Notification: After using Apple Pay and providing your rewards card details, you might receive a notification on your iPhone prompting you to add the card as a rewards card. Tap the notification and select "Add."
- Message: Simply tap a rewards card sent to you in Messages.

USING A REWARDS CARD ON APPLE WATCH

When asked to provide your rewards information (and upon seeing the Apple Pay logo), follow these steps:
1. Double-click the side button on your Apple Watch.
2. Hold your watch a few centimeters away from the contactless reader, with the display facing the reader.

By default, your Apple Watch displays the rewards card, eliminating the need to scroll.

MAKING APPLE PAY PURCHASES ON MAC WITH APPLE WATCH

For websites supporting Apple Pay, you can initiate a purchase in Safari on your Mac and finalize the payment using your Apple Watch.
To authenticate payments on your Apple Watch, ensure that your iPhone and Mac share the same Apple ID for iCloud. Both your Mac and Apple Watch should also be in proximity and connected to Wi-Fi.

SHOPPING ON MAC AND PAYING WITH APPLE WATCH

1. While shopping online in Safari on your Mac, select the Apple Pay option during checkout.
2. Review payment, shipping, and billing details on your Mac. Make sure it indicates "Confirm with Apple Watch."
3. If the confirmation message appears, double-click the side button on your Apple Watch to complete the payment.

DISABLING APPLE PAY PAYMENTS ON MAC

By default, you can confirm Apple Pay transactions made on your Mac using your Apple Watch. You can do this by:
1. Open the Apple Watch app on your iPhone.
2. Go to "My Watch," then "Wallet & Apple Pay."
3. Turn off "Allow Payments on Mac."

USING TRANSIT CARDS WITH APPLE WATCH

On your Apple Watch, you can utilize a transit card through Apple Pay to pay for fares where applicable. Refer to the Apple Support article "Ride transit with Apple Pay" for more details. Note that Apple Pay availability and features may vary by location.

If a preferred card is not required by a transit system, you can use a payment card in Wallet for transit payment without double-clicking the side button. To set up a card for Express Transit:
1. Open the Settings app on your Apple Watch.
2. Navigate to "Wallet & Apple Pay," then select "Express Mode."
3. Choose the card you wish to use, enter your Apple Watch passcode, and follow the instructions for payment.

USING YOUR DRIVER'S LICENSE OR STATE ID IN WALLET ON IPHONE AND APPLE WATCH (U.S. ONLY)

ADDING YOUR LICENSE OR ID

You can securely and conveniently add your driver's license or state ID to the Wallet app on your iPhone and Apple Watch. This allows you to present your license or ID at specific TSA security checkpoints using either device. (Note that the license or ID must be issued by a participating state.)
Adding Your License or ID to iPhone and Apple Watch

1. Open the Wallet app on your iPhone.
2. Tap the button .
3. Choose "Driver's License" or "State ID" and then select your state.
• If your state isn't listed, it might not be participating yet.

4. Decide if you want to add the license or ID to your iPhone only or both iPhone and paired Apple Watch.
4. Follow the onscreen instructions to scan the front and back of your license or ID.

USING YOUR LICENSE OR ID ON APPLE WATCH

1. Hold your Apple Watch display near the identity reader.
2. Review the information to be shared.
3. Double-click the side button on your Apple Watch to present your license or ID.
- A checkmark appears when your license or ID is successfully presented.

To use your license or ID on your Apple Watch, you must unlock your iPhone using Face ID or Touch ID each time you put on your watch. Afterward, you can use the license or ID without further authentication until you remove the watch.

ACCESSING CAR, HOME, WORKPLACE, AND HOTEL KEYS IN WALLET

In the Wallet app on your Apple Watch, you can store keys for your car, home, and hotel room.

UNLOCKING AND STARTING YOUR CAR

With a compatible car and digital car key in Apple Wallet, you can unlock, lock, and start your car using your iPhone or Apple Watch (Series 6 and later). Ultra Wideband ensures that you can't lock your device in the car.

UNLOCKING YOUR HOME

For HomeKit-compatible smart locks, you can unlock your door using a home key in Apple Wallet on supported devices. Add a home key through the Home app on your iPhone.

ACCESSING YOUR WORKPLACE

If your workplace participates, add your corporate access badge to the Wallet app. To access badge-secured areas, hold your iPhone or Apple Watch near the reader.

UNLOCKING YOUR HOTEL ROOM

At participating hotels, add your room key to Apple Wallet using the hotel app, check in remotely, and use your iPhone or Apple Watch to unlock your room.

USING COVID-19 VACCINATION CARDS IN WALLET ON APPLE WATCH

With iOS 15 or newer, you have the option to securely download verifiable COVID-19 vaccination and lab records. These records are stored in the Health app on your iPhone. Once downloaded, it's easy to add the vaccination record to your Wallet app on iPhone. This record is then automatically synchronized with your Apple Watch (requires iOS 15.1 and watchOS 8.1 or later). This feature is supported by certain healthcare providers and authorities. You can then present your vaccination card stored in your Wallet app as proof of vaccination.

SHOWING YOUR VACCINATION CARD

To present your vaccination card using your Apple Watch, follow these steps:
1. Double-click the side button on your Apple Watch.
2. Scroll to locate your vaccination card.
3. Tap the card to open it and reveal the QR code.
4. Show the QR code to the reader as required. Depending on the situation, you might be asked to verify your identity by showing an official photo ID, like your driver's license.

REVIEWING YOUR CARD INFORMATION:

If you need to review the information stored on your vaccination card, simply follow these steps:
1. Scroll down within the card details.
2. Tap "Pass Information" to access additional information.

WEATHER

CHECKING THE WEATHER

You can easily get weather updates on your Apple Watch using Siri. Just say something like, "What's tomorrow's forecast for Honolulu?"

Turn to see more weather information.

Tap to see temperature or precipitation forecast.

VIEWING WEATHER CONDITIONS

To check weather conditions, follow these steps:
1. Open the Weather app on your Apple Watch.
2. Tap on a city to see the current temperature and conditions for the day.
3. Tap the display to cycle through hourly forecasts for rain, conditions, or temperature.
4. Scroll down to view air quality, UV index, wind speed, humidity, visibility information, and a 10-day forecast.
5. Tap the "<" in the top-left corner to return to the list

ADDING A CITY

To add a new city to your weather list:
1. Open the Weather app on your Apple Watch.
2. Scroll to the bottom of the list and tap "Add City."
3. Enter the city name using Scribble, dictation, or type it directly (for Apple Watch Series 7 and 8).
4. Tap "Search" and select the city name from the results.

REMOVING A CITY

To remove a city from your list:
1. Open the Weather app 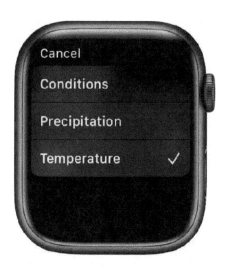.
2. Swipe the city you want to remove to the left, then tap "X."

CHANGING WEATHER METRICS

You can choose the metric displayed below each city:
1. Open the Weather app .
2. Tap "Viewing" at the top of the screen.
3. Choose "Conditions," "Precipitation," or "Temperature."

SETTING DEFAULT CITY

1. Open the Settings app on your Apple Watch.
2. Go to "Weather," then tap "Default City."
3. Choose a city from the list you added on your iPhone or Apple Watch.

WEATHER ADVISORIES

If there's a significant weather event, you might receive a notification at the top of the Weather app. Tap "Learn More" to get further details about the event.

WORKOUT

USING THE WORKOUT APP

The Workout app 🏃 on your Apple Watch is a great tool to manage your workout sessions. It allows you to set specific goals like time, distance, or calories for your workouts. Your progress is tracked, and your results are summarized. You can also review your complete workout history using the Fitness app on your iPhone.

ENHANCEMENTS IN WATCHOS 9

On previous models, the workout app has some features listed through this guide, this will be detailed in the following page along with the Apple watchOS 9 new enhancements including:

- Heart Rate Zones: Monitor workout intensity with automatic or manually created Heart Rate Zones.
- New Workout Views: View important metrics like Activity rings, Heart Rate Zones, Running Power, Elevation, Splits, and segments by turning the Digital Crown.
- New Running Metrics: Running form metrics like Stride Length, Ground Contact Time, and Vertical Oscillation are available as metrics in Workout Views (for Apple Watch SE and Series 6 and later).
- Custom Workouts: Customize work and recovery intervals with alerts for pace, heart rate, cadence, and power.
- Multisport Workout: Easily switch between workouts like triathlons using auto-detection.
- Running Power: Measure your running effort in watts and maintain a sustainable level (for Apple Watch SE and Series 6 and later).
- Race Route: Race against your previous or best result in an Outdoor Run or Outdoor Cycle workout.
- Automatic Track Detection: When starting an Outdoor Run at a track, you're prompted to begin a Track workout with lane options and lap alerts.
- Swimming Enhancements: Pool Swim workouts now detect a kickboard stroke type and track efficiency with SWOLF score.

STARTING A WORKOUT

Tap to set workout goals.

Turn the Digital Crown to choose another workout.

TO START A WORKOUT ON YOUR

APPLE WATCH

1. Open the Workout app 🏃.
2. Turn the Digital Crown to choose your workout type.
3. Tap "Add Workout" at the bottom for special sessions.
4. Tap the desired workout and start.

You can also ask Siri to start a workout, like "Start a 30-minute run" or "Go for a 5-mile walk."

SETTING A PACE FOR OUTDOOR RUN:

You can set a target pace for an outdoor run:
1. Open the Workout app 🏃.
2. Choose "Outdoor Run" and tap ● ● ● "Create Workout," then select "Pacer."
3. Adjust the distance and target time.

Your watch displays your average and current pace, and whether you're ahead or behind your chosen pace.

USING RACE ROUTE

For familiar routes, race against your previous or best time:
1. Open the Workout app 🏃.
2. Tap ● ● ● next to an Outdoor Run or Cycle.
3. Choose "Race Route," then select "Last" or "Personal Best."

Your watch shows your progress compared to the route and remaining distance.

COMBINING ACTIVITIES IN A SINGLE WORKOUT

1. Open the Workout app 🏃 on your Apple Watch.
2. Start your first workout, like an outdoor run.
3. When you want to switch to a different activity, such as an outdoor bike ride, swipe right, tap the ✛ icon, and choose the new workout.
4. Once you've finished all activities, swipe right and tap "End."
5. Use the Digital Crown to navigate through the results summary.
6. Scroll to the bottom and tap "Done" to save the workout.

Note: Built-in GPS allows accurate distance tracking during outdoor workouts, so you can leave your iPhone at home.

CREATING A MULTISPORT WORKOUT

With a Multisport workout, combine running, cycling, and swimming activities. Your Apple Watch detects switches between these activities.

1. Open the Workout app 🏃 on your Apple Watch.
2. Depending on if it's your first Multisport workout or not:
   - First Multisport workout: Tap the Multisport workout, then "Create Workout."
   - Subsequent workouts: Tap the ••• icon, then "Create Workout."
3. Add activities (e.g., Outdoor Run) by tapping "Add" for each.
4. Configure alerts and activity order by tapping each activity. Reorder activities by dragging.
5. Customize Workout Views for each activity.
6. Name the workout by tapping "Untitled" and entering a name.
7. Choose automatic/manual transitions between activities under "Transitions."
8. Save the Multisport workout by tapping "Create Workout."
9. To start a Multisport workout, open the app, scroll to the Multisport workout, tap the ✛ icon, and choose a workout.
10. To delete a Multisport workout, tap the Multisport workout tile, tap the ⊘ icon next to the workout, scroll down, tap "Delete Workout," then confirm "Delete."

ADJUSTING APPLE WATCH DURING A WORKOUT

While working out, make the most of your Apple Watch:
- Raise your wrist to view workout stats like time, pace, distance, calories burned, and heart rate. Turn the Digital Crown for more views.

- Pause and resume by pressing the side button and Digital Crown together or by swiping right and tapping "Pause" (except for swimming).
- Mark workout segments by double-tapping the display.
- Control music and volume by swiping left for the Now Playing screen.
- To enable or disable Voice Feedback, open Settings ⚙ on your Apple Watch, go to Workouts, then Voice Feedback.

AUTOMATIC TRACK WORKOUTS ON APPLE WATCH

With the newest update, your Apple Watch seamlessly recognizes when you're at a track. During an Outdoor Run workout, your watch suggests a start Tracking workout option.

STARTING A TRACK WORKOUT

1. Open the Workout app 🏃 on your Apple Watch.
2. Select "Outdoor Run."
   - If your watch detects that you're at a track, it prompts you to choose a lane.
3. Tap "Choose Lane," adjust your lane using the plus/minus buttons, then tap "Confirm."
4. If it's your first Track workout, select a measurement unit (Miles or Meters), then confirm.

To modify the measurement unit later, navigate to the Settings app ⚙ then Workout > Units of Measure, and choose a unit under Track Workouts.
Your Apple Watch informs you if you leave or arrive at a track mid-workout, ensuring accurate tracking.

ENABLING LAP ALERTS

Receive alerts displaying distance, time, and pace for each track lap:
1. Tap ••• next to "Outdoor Run," then tap 🖊 next to any goal.
2. Tap "Alerts," turn the Digital Crown upwards, select "Track Lap," and enable "Lap Alert."

LANE ADJUSTMENT DURING A WORKOUT

If you change lanes during your workout:
Swipe right on the watch face, tap "Lane," and enter the new lane.

ENDING AND REVIEWING YOUR WORKOUT

When you achieve your goal, a tone and vibration signal completion. If you wish to continue, your Apple Watch continues gathering data until you stop it.
1. Swipe right, then tap "End."
2. Use the Digital Crown to navigate the results summary, then tap "Done" at the bottom.

Note: The heart rate sensor remains active for three minutes post-workout to measure recovery.*

WORKOUT REVIEW

1. Open the Health app  on your iPhone.
2. Tap "Summary," then select a workout.

The summary includes workout specifics, splits, heart rate, and route. Tap "Show More" next to each item for detailed information.

For route tracking, enable it during initial setup or later in:
*   Apple Watch: Settings app ⚙️> Privacy > Location Services > Apple Watch Workout > While Using the App.
*   iPhone: Settings > Privacy > Location Services > Apple Watch Workout > While Using the App.

Note: To view a specific workout type, tap "Show More" beside Workouts, select the type, and to return to all workouts, tap the workout name and "All Workouts."

CUSTOMIZE YOUR WORKOUTS ON APPLE WATCH

ADJUSTING WORKOUT GOALS

Personalize your workouts on Apple Watch to match your fitness aspirations. Tailor time, calorie, and distance targets, incorporate warmup and cooldown periods, and include work and recovery intervals.

MODIFYING GOALS

In watchOS 9, customizing existing workouts and crafting your desired workout is easy:
1. Open the Workout app 🏃 on your Apple Watch.
2. Scroll to your chosen workout.
3. Tap • • •, then select "Create Workout."
4. Opt for a goal like Calories, Distance, or Time; set a value; and tap "Done."
5. Start the edited workout by tapping the adjusted goal.
6. You can also tap < to save the edited workout and begin later.

To remove edited goals from a workout, scroll to the workout, tap• • •, tap ⊘ next to the goal, scroll down, tap "Delete Workout," and confirm deletion.

ADDING INTERVALS

Tailor your workouts with warmup, work, recovery, and cooldown intervals:
1. Open the Workout app 🏃 on your Apple Watch.
2. Choose your desired workout.
3. Tap • • •, scroll to the bottom, and tap "Create Workout."
4. Opt for "Custom," and perform the following:
   - Add a warmup: Tap Warmup, select Time, Distance, or Open, and add a heart rate alert if desired.
   - Incorporate work and recovery intervals: Tap Add, tap Work or Recovery, and choose Time, Distance, or Open. You can include multiple intervals.
   - Add a cooldown: Tap Cooldown, choose Time, Distance, or Open. With "Open," you can include a heart rate alert.
   - Name the workout: Tap "Untitled" below Custom Title and enter a name.
   Note:For stationary workouts like Elliptical or Pilates, Distance isn't available.

5. Tap "Create Workout." This button is active if a work or recovery interval is added.
6.
To remove warmup or cooldown periods, tap • • •next to the workout, tap 🖊 within the Custom tile, tap Warmup or Cooldown, and tap "Skip." For work or recovery intervals, tap the interval, then tap "Delete Interval."

Custom workouts apply to all workout types except Multisport, Pool Swim, and Open Water Swim.

ADDING ALERTS

Receive various alerts during workouts, such as heart rate alerts:
1. Open the Workout app 🏃 on your Apple Watch.
2. Choose the workout.
3. Tap • • •, tap the edit button for a tile, and tap "Alerts."
4. Opt for an alert, configure it, and these added alerts apply to future instances of that workout.

VIEWING HEART RATE ZONES

In watchOS 9, monitor your cardio-focused workout intensity by viewing Heart Rate Zone data on your Apple Watch. Heart Rate Zones are calculated from your health data, showing effort levels from light to challenging.

VIEWING ZONES DURING A WORKOUT

1. Open the Workout app 🏃 on your Apple Watch.
2. Begin a cardio-focused workout, like an outdoor run.
3. Scroll to the Heart Rate Zone workout view using the Digital Crown.

The display showcases your Heart Rate Zone, heart rate, time in the current zone, and average heart rate.

REVIEWING ZONE DATA

1. Open the Fitness app 💜 on your iPhone.
2. Select a workout and tap Show More next to Heart Rate.
A graph illustrates the time spent in each zone.

EDITING ZONES

While Heart Rate Zones are usually calculated from health data, you can manually adjust them:
1. Open the Settings app ⚙ on your Apple Watch.
2. Navigate to Workout > Heart Rate Zones.
3. Choose Manual, select a zone (2, 3, or 4), and input upper and lower limits.

Alternatively, use the Apple Watch app on your iPhone. Tap My Watch, go to Workout > Heart Rate Zones, opt for Manual, select a zone, and input limits.
Viewing and Customizing Workout Metrics on Apple Watch:

TRACKING YOUR PROGRESS

Apple Watch provides valuable metrics such as active calories, heart rate, and distance during workouts to help you monitor your performance. Each workout type displays default metrics relevant to the activity, which you can personalize.

SWITCHING VIEWS

During a workout, simply turn the Digital Crown to cycle through different workout views.

PERSONALIZING VIEWS

The workout views depend on your chosen activity. Cardio-focused workouts feature more default views, but you can customize some of them to match your workout preferences.

1. Open the Workout app 🏃 on your Apple Watch.
2. Scroll to your selected workout.
3. Tap • • •, tap ⊘ within any tile, then tap "Workout Views."
4. Choose "Edit Views," browse through the workout views, and tap "Include" next to the metrics you want to appear.
5. For the first two workout views, select metrics by tapping ⊘ in the Metric 1 or Metric 2 set, and choosing a different metric.

ENHANCING YOUR RUNNING METRICS

In watchOS 9, Apple Watch offers insights into your running form and power:
- Vertical oscillation: Vertical movement with each step, measured in cm.
- Ground contact time: Time foot is on the ground while running, measured in ms.
- Stride length: Distance per step, measured in meters.
- Running power: Output of work while running, measured in watts.

OUTDOOR RUN METRICS

The Outdoor Run workout presents various metrics:
- Metric 1: Current heart rate, rolling mile, average pace, distance
- Metric 2: Running cadence, stride length, ground contact time, vertical oscillation
- Heart Rate Zones: Current heart rate, time in zone, average heart rate
- Split: Split number, split pace, split distance, current heart rate
- Segment: Segment number, segment pace, segment distance, current heart rate
- Elevation: Elevation profile, elevation gained, current elevation
- Power: Power profile, current power, average power
- Activity rings: Move, exercise & stand.

SWIM EFFICIENTLY

In watchOS 9, Pool Swim workouts feature kickboard detection and SWOLF scores, combining stroke count with time for one pool length.

STARTING A SWIM WORKOUT

1. Open the Workout app 🏃 on your Apple Watch.
2. Choose Open Water Swim or Pool Swim.

Pause or resume your swim by pressing the Digital Crown and side button together. Water Lock engages when swimming to prevent accidental interactions. After swimming, press and hold the Digital Crown to unlock the screen and clear any water from the speaker.

VIEWING SWIM SUMMARY

Unlock your Apple Watch and tap End to see your swim workout summary. It tracks sets, rest periods, stroke types, and total distance. Set paces are visible in your iPhone's workout summary.

CLEARING WATER MANUALLY

1. Swipe up on the screen to open Control Center, then tap 💧 .
2. Hold the Digital Crown to clear water from the speaker after swimming.

USING GYM EQUIPMENT WITH APPLE WATCH

Apple Watch can sync data with compatible cardio equipment like treadmills, ellipticals, and indoor bikes, providing accurate workout insights.

Pairing Your Watch

Follow these steps to pair your Apple Watch with gym equipment:

1. Check for compatibility—look for "Connects to Apple Watch" on the equipment.
2. Ensure your watch detects gym equipment: Open Settings ⚙ on your Apple Watch, tap Workout, and enable Detect Gym Equipment.
3. Hold your Apple Watch close to the contactless reader on the equipment with the display facing it. A tap and beep indicate successful pairing.

STARTING AND ENDING A WORKOUT

Begin by pressing "Start" on the equipment and end by pressing "Stop." Workout data integrates into the Activity app on your Apple Watch and the Fitness app on your iPhone.

UPDATING YOUR PROFILE

For accurate calculations, update your height, weight, sex, age, and wheelchair status:
1. Open the Apple Watch app on your iPhone.
2. Go to My Watch, select Health > Health Details, and tap Edit.
3. Adjust Height or Weight as needed.

CALIBRATING FOR ACCURACY

Your Apple Watch uses your profile and GPS for accurate metrics. If you run with your iWatch, the app calibrates your stride for distance accuracy.

CHANGING MEASUREMENT UNITS

Adjust the Workout app's measurement units to your preference:
1. Open Settings on your Apple Watch.
2. Tap Workout, scroll down, and tap Units of Measure to change energy, pool length, cycling, walking, and running units.

AUTO-PAUSE AND MANUAL PAUSING

Enable Auto-Pause for outdoor running and cycling workouts to pause and resume automatically. Manually pause using the side button and Digital Crown.

WORKOUT REMINDERS

Receive prompts to start the Workout app during activities like walking, running, and swimming:
1. Open Settings on your Apple Watch.
2. Tap Workout, and adjust Start and End Workout Reminder settings.

CONSERVING POWER

Prolong battery life during workouts by activating Low Power Mode:
1. Open Settings on your Apple Watch.
2. Tap Workout, and enable Low Power Mode.

During workouts, Low Power Mode conserves energy by turning off certain features. To further save battery life, turn off GPS and Heart Rate Readings.

WORLD CLOCK

Apple Watch's World Clock feature lets you view time across various cities.

ADDING AND REMOVING CITIES

Here's how to add and remove cities in World Clock:
1. Open World Clock  on your Apple Watch.
2. Tap Add City.
3. Enter the city name using Scribble or dictation (available on Apple Watch Series 7 and 8).
4. Tap the city name to add it. To remove a city, swipe left and tap X.

Cities added on your iPhone appear on your Apple Watch too.

CHECKING TIME IN OTHER CITIES

1. Open World Clock 🌐 on your Apple Watch.
2. Use the Digital Crown or swipe to scroll through the list.
3. Tap a city to see additional info like sunrise and sunset times.
4. Tap < or swipe right to return to the city list.

You can also add a World Clock complication to your watch face for quick access.

CHANGING CITY ABBREVIATIONS

To alter city abbreviations on your Apple Watch
1. Open the Apple Watch app 🔘 on your iPhone.
2. Go to My Watch, then Clock > City Abbreviations.
3. Change an abbreviation by tapping a city.

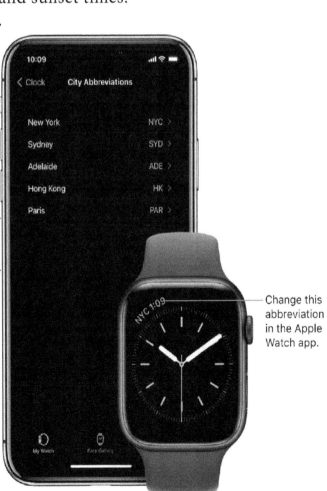

Change this abbreviation in the Apple Watch app.

UPDATE, BACKUP, RESTORE & RESET YOUR IWATCH

Recovering and Managing Apple Watch

Apple provides regular updates to your IOS so your iPhone in tip top condition working like it's brand new. Software updates can contain major or minor changes depending on the version. You can update your iPhone manually and set it to "Automatic Update" which allows your phone to download and install new software as it comes out.

Digital Crown

Side button

RECOVER APPLE WATCH

If your Apple Watch displays an animation of a watch and iPhone brought together, follow these steps:

1. Position your iPhone close to your Apple Watch.
   Ensure your iPhone is running iOS 15.4 or later, connected to Wi-Fi with Bluetooth on, and unlocked.
2. Place your Apple Watch on its charger.
3. Double-click the side button on your Apple Watch, then follow the prompts on the iPhone.

RESTORE APPLE WATCH FROM BACKUP

Your Apple Watch automatically backs up to your paired iPhone, allowing restoration from a backup. These backups are included in your iPhone's backup—whether to iCloud, Mac, or PC. iCloud backups can't be directly viewed.

BACKUP AND RESTORATIO

- Backup: When paired with an iPhone, Apple Watch content continuously backs up to the iPhone. Unpairing devices initiates a backup. For details, see "Back up your Apple Watch" on Apple Support.
- Restore from Backup: Pairing your Apple Watch with the same iPhone or getting a new Apple Watch lets you choose "Restore from Backup" and select a stored backup on your

iPhone.

Managed family member's Apple Watch backs up to their iCloud account while connected to power and Wi-Fi. To disable iCloud backups, navigate to Settings > [account name] > iCloud > iCloud Backups on the managed watch, then disable iCloud Backups.

UPDATING APPLE WATCH SOFTWARE

Easily update your Apple Watch software via the Apple Watch app on your iPhone.

CHECK AND INSTALL UPDATES

1. Open the Apple Watch app on your iPhone.
2. Access My Watch, go to General > Software Update, and if available, tap Download and Install.

Alternatively, go to Settings app on your Apple Watch, then navigate to General > Software Update.

FORGOT APPLE WATCH PASSCODE

If your Apple Watch is disabled due to forgotten or repeatedly incorrect passcodes, use the Apple Watch app on your iPhone to re-enter the passcode. If still forgotten, reset your Apple Watch and set it up again.

Important: If Erase Data is enabled, after 10 unsuccessful attempts, your Apple Watch data is erased.

UNLOCK MORE POSSIBILITIES WITH OUR COMPANION GUIDE!

If you've enjoyed mastering your Apple Watch with "Apple Watch for Seniors: A Simple Step-by-Step Guide," you're going to love our "iPhone for Seniors - A Simple Step by Step Guide for Beginners."

Discover how to effortlessly navigate your iPhone, from sending messages to capturing memories and everything in between. This comprehensive guide is designed to empower beginners to embrace the world of smartphones with confidence.

Ready to embark on another journey of tech enlightenment?

Get your copy of "iPhone for Seniors" today and continue your exploration of everything apple!

Open this QR code on your iPhone and grab your copy now!

www.ingramcontent.com/pod-product-compliance
Lightning Source LLC
LaVergne TN
LVHW081757050326
832903LV00027B/1991